Eyewitnesses
at the
Battle of Stones River

David R. Logsdon
2711 Barclay Dr., Nashville, TN 37206

Cover layout by Linda Walters.
Cover illustration, map, and drawings on pages 6, 18, 27, 56 and 62 from "Battles and Leaders of the Civil War."
Drawings on pages 2, 3, 22, 33, 45 and 58 from "Harper's New Monthly Magazine" and "Harper's Pictorial History of the Civil War."

The Battlefield and Related Sites

Stones River National Battlefield is open from 8 a.m. to 5 p.m. daily, and there are no admittance or special use charges.

The self-guided driving tour of the park includes stops where the Chicago Board of Trade Battery and another artillery unit halted a Confederate attack aimed at seizing the Old Nashville Highway, thereby cutting the Union Army off from Nashville; Gen. Philip H. Sheridan's desperate stand in the cedars, which gave Rosecrans time to form a new line on the Old Nashville Highway; the Round Forest, called "Hell's Half Acre" and "The Slaughter Pen" by survivors; and McFadden's Ford, site of Confederate Gen. John Breckinridge's disastrous charge.

For more information about the park, write to Stones River National Battlefield, Route 10, Box 495, Old Nashville Highway, Murfreesboro, TN 37130 (615-893-9501).

Other Civil War sites nearby include Oaklands Mansion (615-893-0022) in Murfreesboro; Confederate hero Sam Davis' plantation home (615-459-2341) in nearby Smyrna; and, 30 miles west of Murfreesboro, the Carter House (615-791-1861) and Carnton Mansion (615-794-0903) of the Battle of Franklin.

Though the Franklin battlefield has not been preserved, much of the battle's atmosphere clings to the Carter House and Carnton Mansion. The Carter House was just inside the Union line where the Confederate assault almost broke through. The home and its outbuildings are among the most battle damaged Civil War structures still standing. While the battle raged, the Carter family and other civilians hid in the cellar. Capt. Tod Carter fell mortally wounded in a charge near his home. He was carried inside after the battle and died a few days later.

Carnton was used as a hospital, and its floors still bear the stains of blood from wounded soldiers and surgeons' improvised tables. The mansion is best known for its back porch, where at least four Confederate generals killed in the battle were laid out prior to their removal to Columbia for burial. After the war, Carnton's owner gave some land near the family cemetery for reburial of the Confederate dead.

Foreword

This is the Battle of Stones River described by more than 60 men, women and youngsters who saw it and survived it.

With two exceptions, nothing has been changed in blending passages from their letters, diaries and memoirs into this unusual "you-are-there" chronological account of the battle. Parentheses enclose a word or phrase inserted for clarity, and ellipses indicate omissions in passages quoted.

My thanks to Stones River National Battlefield historian Charles M. Spearman for helping me track down sources and for answering questions about sequences of events. A map sold at the park was an invaluable guide in keeping up with eyewitnesses' movements.

If you notice any points of confusion, please contact me so they can be clarified in the next edition.

I would also appreciate being alerted to other good first-person accounts that could make subsequent editions of "Eyewitnesses at the Battle of Stones River" better.

David R. Logsdon
2711 Barclay Dr.
Nashville, TN 37206

615-226-0638

Who Won?

The Battle of Stones River began at dawn, December 31, 1862, when Braxton Bragg's 37,700 Confederates attacked William Rosecrans' 43,400 Union troops just north of Murfreesboro, Tennessee. There was little fighting on New Year's Day, and the lull lasted till late in the afternoon of January 2, when Bragg hurled Gen. John Breckinridge's division against the Union left flank in a charge that cost the Confederates more 1,700 casualties.

After the battle, both sides claimed it as a victory. Rosecrans held the battlefield, but Bragg had inflicted losses of 12,706 (1,636 killed; 7,397 wounded; 3,673 prisoners) while suffering only 9,870 casualties (1,236 killed; 7,766 wounded; 898 prisoners).

But, Stones River was much more important to the Union's ultimate victory in the Civil War than possession of the battlefield or comparisons of casualties, J.T. Gibson, a veteran of the battle, noted in his history of the 78th Pennsylvania:

> "Before this battle took place the outlook for our country was very dark and threatening.
>
> "Our armies had gained no signal victories for many months, and there was very great danger that some of the Nations of Europe would recognize the Southern Confederacy, and that it would be impossible for us to maintain our blockade.
>
> "Had General Rosecrans' Army been defeated at the Battle of Stone River, and compelled to retire to Nashville, it would not only have prolonged the War, but would have greatly increased our danger of becoming involved in conflicts with foreign countries."

Contents

BATTLE-FIELDS OF STONE'S RIVER TENN.

Dec. 31-Jan. 3 1862-3

EXPLANATION

UNION — *First Position of Troops* — CONFEDERATE

Last " " "

SCALE OF MILES

½ 1 2

J. WELLS

The Round Forest mentioned in the text included the right of Harker's first position and all of Hazen's position, field of December 31st.

The Target

"Murfreesboro is situated on high rolling ground on the right bank of Stone River about thirty miles from Nashville. Previous to the war it claimed a population of five thousand. It is the center of a rich agricultural district, and from it diverge many turnpikes and roads communicating with the principal places in middle Tennessee."

---J.T. Gibson, 78th Pennsylvania, Miller's Brigade

(In the spring of 1862 Union troops briefly occupied Murfreesboro, and the civilians' sharp class distinctions impressed an officer who would command a brigade during the Battle of Stones River:)

"Murfreesboro is an aristocratic town. Many of the citizens have as fine carriages as are to be seen in Cincinnati or Washington. On pleasant week-day evenings they sometimes come out to witness the parades. The ladies, so far as I can judge by a glimpse through a carriage window, are richly and elegantly dressed.

"The poor whites are as poor as rot, and the rich are very rich. There is no substantial well-to-do middle class. The slaves are, in fact, the middle class here. They are not considered so good, of course, as their masters, but a great deal better than the white trash.

...

"The colored people of Murfreesboro pour out in great numbers on Sunday evenings to witness dress parade. Some of them in excellent holiday attire. The women sport flounces and the men canes. Many are nearly white, and all are slaves."

---Col. John Beatty, commander 3rd Ohio

Rebels Give Ground

(In the winter of 1862 the Union Army of the Cumberland is camped in and around Nashville, Tennessee's capital. About 30 miles to the south, the Confederate Army of Tennessee is in camps scattered around Murfreesboro.

(Gen. Braxton Bragg apparently expects the Yankees to stay put for a while. His scouts do not detect the accumulation of supplies and reinforcements in Nashville, but the Rebel horsemen keep Union patrols from learning much about the location of units of Bragg's army.

(However, the Union high command is in no mood to let Rebel troops dispute control of Middle Tennessee. The Army of the Cumberland's commander, William Rosecrans, is under pressure to take the offensive:)

Murfreesboro

"By the middle of December the Louisville and Nashville Railroad had been repaired, and by the 20th sufficient provisions had been accumulated to support the Army until navigation should be opened on the Cumberland River. ... From the 12th of December until the 26th time was devoted to drilling and disciplining the troops and perfecting the organization of the Army. Foraging parties went out nearly every day and they generally reported skirmishes with the enemy. Reconnoitering parties also went out on all the principal roads leading in the direction of Murfreesboro ... to ascertain the position and the strength of the enemy."

---Gibson, 78th Pennsylvania, Miller's Brigade

"My home was between the two armies, ... twelve miles from Murfreesboro. ... Scouting parties, making petty fights and movements, and foraging parties of both sides, made things lively, and an occasional gathering of the young folks between the lines ... lent a lively pastime to some of our soldiers. ... As one ... too young to be called for service, the limit being 18, I would go along with the soldier boys ... and join in the revelry."

---Bromfield Ridley, civilian

(In late December, Rosecrans is ready to launch an offensive, and he orders the Army of the Cumberland south to clear the Rebels out of Murfreesboro:)

"The morning of (Friday) December 26th was cloudy and misty, but the reveille sounded an hour before day; tents were 'struck,' and at break of day the army moved forward in three columns, the right wing under General McCook, advancing by the Nolensville Pike to Triune; the center, under General Thomas, by the Franklin and Wilson Pikes to Nolensvile, and the left wing, under General Crittenden, by the Murfreesboro pike to Lavergne. ... It rained almost incessantly, and the roads were very muddy."

---Gibson, 78th Pennsylvania, Miller's Brigade

"The country was hilly and rough, with thickets of cedar, intersected by small streams, with rocky, bluff banks. The road was rough and muddy, and it was only by the utmost efforts that the teams could be got through. General Negley, our division commander, frequently alighting from his horse, pulling off his coat, and rolling up his sleeves, would assist the teamsters in pulling through. Several times Colonel Moody would become impatient, urging us on as we struggled through the mud and rain, telling us that the fight would be over before we got there, as ever and anon we could hear the boom of cannon in advance of us. But I guess the colonel got enough of it."

---Ira A. Owens, 74th Ohio, Miller's Brigade

(Meanwhile, at Readyville, a small community 14 miles east of Murfreesboro, a Texas artillery commander treats himself to an outing after staying in camp Christmas Day to let his lieutenants attend a dinner. The officer is angry with his girlfriend in Texas. He hasn't gotten any letters from her lately, so he concludes she has ditched him:)

"On the 26th (I) rode out in the country 5 or 6 miles. ... Stopped at a large mansion near the road and found an old motherly lady the principal inhabitant. ... Two very pretty (young women) ... made their appearances in the parlor. ... One of the young ladies was named Lucy Haskins ... pretty and intelligent. ...

"I found it to be their purpose to visit Readyville, and ... I ventured to accompany them. It was raining, but ... we mounted and rode away. The rain fell faster and finally poured, but on we sped full speed until we took up cold and wet at the residence of one of the young ladies' relatives. ...

"I enjoyed a good fire in a comfortable home for an hour or two, when dinner was announced. The young ladies, looking fresh and dry, came out and after ... a good Christmas dinner we arranged ourselves around the center table and engaged in a game of Euchre.

"I told Miss Lucy I had a sweetheart in Texas but that she had not written to me for a long time. Lucy said she had a sweetheart in the army but she feared he would be killed, and I inferred she would take another string to her bow.

"Thus the time was passing agreeably when a rumbling sound came over the distant hills. ... We soon recognized it as the roar of cannons, but the game went on."

---Capt. James P. Douglas, Douglas' Texas Battery, Ector's Brigade

"We did not strike any enemy until near night, when we got near a little town, Nolensville, fifteen miles or about half way to Murfreesborough. There we had quite a little skirmish with the Rebel Cavalry. ... We had to bring up a brigade or two of Infantry but we soon routed them and took the town and also captured ... (two guns)."

---Alexander C. Pepper, 59th Illinois, Post's Brigade

"Lucy ... grew a little pale as peal succeeded peal, and we could distinguish that the battle was drawing nearer and the roar of the cannon becoming more constant. We played on and kept count of our points and marches, but Lucy would sigh occasionally. Thus went the evening. ... I parted with Lucy and her friends, promising to call again and she promising to call and see my guns.

"I returned to camp and gave orders with a view to an early movement. Sure enough, at midnight we were aroused by orders from General Bragg to move immediately to Murfreesboro, a distance of 14 miles. We were soon on the road ... the mud and water under foot, and the pelting rain over head. I, that night, traversed the same road on the march to battle which I had bounded over the day before with so much pleasure in company with Lucy and her friend."

---Capt. Douglas, Douglas' Texas Battery, Ector's Brigade

(Bragg also sends for a brigade camped far to the southeast, near the junction of the Tennessee, Alabama and Georgia state lines:)

"My husband, ... (was) a captain ... on the staff of Brig. Gen. John K. Jackson, whose brigade was stationed at Bridgeport, Ala. ... We had enjoyed our Christmas dinner, such as it was, two days before. Like a thunderclap out of a clear sky came the orders (Sunday, Dec. 28) to move at once and join Gen. Bragg's army, as Rosecrans was threatening to attack it near Murfreesboro. ...

"It was a great relief when Mrs. Jackson said, 'I've decided to go with the troops as far as Wartrace, (Tennessee,) where I have relatives,' and, turning to me, 'you must come, too, for they are such loyal Confederates. I know they will cheerfully take in any one whose husband is in the army.' ... I gladly accepted. ...

"We took a hastily improvised train, and about four o'clock that wintry afternoon it stopped at a small desolate station, about eighteen miles from Murfreesboro, and deposited our forlorn little party and trunks on the platform, ... where there were no signs of life. The train sped on its way, dwindling to a speck in the distance, while with

heavy hearts ... we watched those nearest and dearest to us borne swiftly away to certain battle. ...

"Night was coming on. ... Mrs. Jackson bestirred herself to find conveyance for ourselves and our belongings ...to the home of her relatives, where, unannounced, we expected to take refuge."

---**Katharine Hubbell Cumming**

(While Mrs. Cumming worries about her husband and how Mrs. Jackson's relatives will receive her and her baby, young B.L. Ridley is at a party at the Smyrna Depot, north of Murfreesboro:)

"It was said that the Federal army was moving upon us; that McCook's Corps had taken the Nashville-Triune pike, Thomas's the

Franklin to the intersection of the Wilson pike, leading to Nolensville, and that Crittendon and Rosecrans were advancing on the pike from Nashville toward Murfreesboro, and had reached Lavergne. The soldiers at the party took leave of their friends and sweethearts. Among them was a lieutenant, F.B. Crosthwait, who went to his command (the 20th Tennessee)."

---Ridley, civilian

"The early-setting December sun disappeared, and it was quite cold. Seeing a fire through the open door of a little one-story house across the wide country road, I took my (10-months-old) baby over there for some warmth. Hesitating at the threshold, I saw a woman with a child stretched out on her lap, apparently ill. She looked up and said: 'You're welcome to come in out of the cold, but my child has scarlet fever.' Any mother will understand my hasty retreat to the windswept platform.

"In the meantime a vehicle had appeared - a one-horse affair without a top - so we jogged along, mostly through the woods, with night upon us, to an unknown place and to people unknown to me."

---Katharine H. Cumming

(The carriage stops at Beechwood, a long, one-story brick plantation house with a porch on either end. The home of Col. Andrew Erwin stretches along a short ridge about a mile and a half south of Wartrace:)

"Col. Erwin and his wife opened their door, as well as their hearts to us. I received as warm a welcome as if I were a dear child returning after an absence. And how inviting that comfortable library and big, crackling wood fire looked. ...

"In this lovely home were ... various people, for no one was turned away who asked shelter. It was hard to tell who were the family proper, as refugee relatives and soldiers on their way to and from 'the front' became unexpected guests like ourselves."

---Katharine Hubbell Cumming

(The Union advance resumes Monday over roads made worse by the steady rain:)

"Our regiment on leaving camp ... marched ... on a dirt road which was very rough and caused great delay to our supply wagons moving ahead of us. The wagons ahead of us would start or stop in frequent intervals ... and we had to follow them in the same way.

"Sometimes the halt would be for a few moments only, again a half (hour) or more would be consumed. We ... were always undecided whether to remain standing in the road or to find a seat on the roadside or even to look for a ... tree to lean against."

---Sgt. Maj. Lyman Widney, 34th Illinois, Kirk's Brigade

(As Rousseau's Division moves through the countryside,

Col. John Beatty is surprised to encounter the teenage daughter of a Mrs. Harris, a staunch secessionist who had asked him for a guard in March, when Union troops occupied the village of Lavergne. Beatty suspected her husband was in the Confederate army, but he provided a guard for the little white cottage:)

"Riding by a farm-house this afternoon, I caught a glimpse of Miss Harris, of Lavergne, at the window, and stopped to talk with her a minute. The young lady and her mother have experienced a great deal of trouble recently. They were shelled out of Lavergne three times, two of the shells passing through her mother's house. She claims to have been shot at once by a soldier of the One Hundred and Nineteenth Illinois, the ball splintering the window-sill near her head. Her mother's house has been converted into a hospital, and the clothes of the famly taken for bandages. She is, therefore, more rebellious now than ever. She is getting her rights, poor girl!"

---Col. J. Beatty, brigade commander

"During the march ... to Murfreesboro, it was nothing but a continual rain day and night, so that we were wet through. The roads were full of mud and slush, so the four days before the fight my feet were wet soaking all the time. (Monday night) all that was left of my shoes gave way, so that I had to go it barefooted."

---Amandus Silsby, 24th Wisconsin, Sill's Brigade

(As Rosecrans' columns converge, Bragg's units deploy to defend the town:)

"Two miles from Murfreesboro ... as the gloom of (Monday) evening was settling, (the Cowan house,) a large brick mansion across the river from us, and in front of Wither's division, was set on fire to be burned out of the way. It was a melancholy sight to see the flames leaping up, and the pillar of inky smoke rising ... from this elegant and once happy home."

---Jonathan S. Jackman, clerk, 9th Kentucky, Hanson's Brigade

"The weather is a cold drizzle (but) we are not permitted to have fires for Genl Bragg does not wish the enemy to be able to locate our line. Beef & corn meal issued to us uncooked & fires not permitted! Col Hunt ordered a detail sent back to the wagons from each company to cook the rations & bring them to us."

---Johnny Green, 9th Kentucky, Hanson's Brigade

"Our cavalry, which had been slowly falling back before the Federal army, burst out from among the cedars in front of Wither's division, and ... came dashing back on our side of the river. Our regiment immediately fell in and advanced in line of battle over a rocky ravine and through an old field where the weeds were up to our shoulders, and so thick we could scarcely move through them. ...

"We halted and sent forward Company 'D' as skirmishers. The company was soon engaged at a lively rate ... in a corn-field on a hill overlooking the river, and ... our regiment was ordered forward to support the skirmish line. Cobb's battery was also moved forward and placed ... on top of the hill, to our right.

"Darkness had now set in, but still the enemy advanced and drove in our skirmishers, the firing being pretty brisk for a time, making the dry cornstalks rattle about us."

---Jackman, 9th Kentucky, Hanson's Brigade

"The yankees ... came with a rush at us in the dark. One volley from our line drove them back however; but our volley brought forth oaths from Mike McClarey, ... who was out on the picket line when our boys were driven in. His comrade was wounded & to bring him home through a corn field where the stalks had not been cut down & take care of his gun at the same time was a difficult task, but with his comrade on his back Mike came swearing at us. ... 'Sure, are you trying to kill your own men?'

"But ... laying his wounded friend down he discovered that a second ball had gone through his head & killed him, whereupon he remarked, 'I thought you said it was your leg you were shot in.' "

---Green, 9th Kentucky, Hanson's Brigade

(Meanwhile, other Union units are trudging along the roads leading to the battlefield north of Murfreesboro:)

"After night set in and it was pitch black ... I was so nearly overcome with sleep that my eyes would close as I walked and dreams would steal into my brain until rudely awakened by the giving away of my knees. ... A halt was worse ... when we stood in our places waiting and expecting to move on in a minute or two. ...

"It was nearly midnight when we reached Wilkinson Cross Roads ... and encamped in a large open field, a distance of 12 miles from our starting point. ... What a relief when we ... crawled into our shelter tents. No fires were allowed as they would disclose our position to the enemy so we were deprived of our coffee but not our slumber."

---Sgt. Maj. Widney, 34th Illinois, Kirk's Brigade

"We got our supper about 12 at night. ... After eating our rations we laid down in line of battle with our guns in our hands to catch a few hours sleep."

---Green, 9th Kentucky, Hanson's Brigade

"Being somewhat a 'soldier at will,' and in poor health, I fell back in good order to a fire in the rear. ... About midnight a heavy rain set in, and I moved into a neighboring corn-crib, where I slept the remainder of the night among the shucks."

---Jackman, 9th Kentucky, Hanson's Brigade

Bragg Diggs In

"At daylight, ... the rain was still pouring down."

---Jackman, 9th Kentucky, Hanson's Brigade

"The army under General Rosecrans kept slightly advancing and taking a more definite position for battle. The skirmishers advanced at different points, discovering masked batteries and rifle pits."

---Gibson, 78th Pennsylvania, Miller's Brigade

"The field of battle was mostly rolling ground, with patches of woodlands. The (Nashville) pike and railroad ran near each other, through the lines of battle, and the ground on the right, where McCook was posted, was a dense succession of cedar thickets, open spaces of rocky ground, belts of timber, and small fields. A number of houses were situated in different parts of the field."

---Owens, 74th Ohio, Miller's Brigade

"When we emerged from the woods, our whole army drew up into line of battle. ... The captain told me to go and stay with the wagons, till I could get a pair of shoes, and a new gun, for my gun had the misfortune of having the tube broken off, the day before. But I, thinking I could get a gun better, by 'hanging around' behind some of the regiments, stopped behind the 15th (Missouri), which was supporting our regiment."

---Silsby, 24th Wisconsin, Sill's Brigade

"(Early Tuesday) morning Gen. Polk ... sent his aide-de-camp, ... (Lt.) William B. Richmond, ordering (a) regiment of infantry to pull down a rail fence which was an obstruction to the movement of troops. ... Richmond rode to the officer in command, Col. (S.S.) Stanton, of the ... (84th) Tennessee ... and transmitted the order.

"Some words passed that led to blows, and though the bullets were flying thick and fast, here was seen the ludicrous spectacle of two officers engaged in a personal fight on the battlefield. Stanton had got Richmond's thumb in his mouth, while Richmond was gnawing away at Stanton's ear. ...

"Finally ... friends parted the belligerents, when they at once resumed their respective posts of duty."

---W.N. Mercer Otey, Gen. Polk's staff

"The Harding Home (south of the Wilkinson Pike) ... at the beginning of the battle of December 30 was just within the enemy's line and in front of Withers's Division. Near this house ... Charles Carroll White, of Company A, (10th South Carolina) won his promotion for distinguished gallantry. ...

"Company A ... was on the right of the picket line of Manigault's Brigade, about half a mile in advance of the main line. ... White, then commanding the company, went down to the right flank of his company to look after it. ... A squadron of the 15th Pennsylvania Cavalry, (under) Major Rosengarten, dashed up and captured Lieutenant White and his two right groups. The Federal major left a squad in charge of the prisoners and galloped on with his squadron.

"Lieutenant White ... called out: ... 'Company A! Rally on the right!' When the men rallied, they hesitated to fire. ... Lieutenant White called out: 'Don't mind us. Fire!' When the fire came, Lieutenant White and the other prisoners grappled their captors and brought them into our line.

"Lieutenant White then formed his company, supported by Company C, of the same regiment, at right angles behind a rail fence. The Federal squadron ... charged on the two companies. ... Major Rosengarten ... rode up to the fence, shot a man in company A with his pistol, but fell riddled himself, and his squadron was easily repulsed. Another squadron of the same regiment made a similar effort, and met like results. ...

"We allowed the Federal surgeon to come through the line to look after their wounded. ... I learned that the Federal loss in killed had been about sixteen, very heavy for a picket affair.

"Immediately on hearing of the incident, General Bragg sent his aide, Captain Parker, to our line with orders to promote Lieutenant White to a captaincy, which was done on the field."

---C. Irving Walker, adjutant general, Manigault's Brigade

(One wounded cavalrymen, Maj. Frank Ward, is taken into a nearby home and cared for by the family. Elsewhere:)

"In afternoon there was heavy cannonading on our left. About 3 oclock sent for one section of our battery - The 1st section commanded by Lieut. (Hardin) ... went - reported to Capt Waters, his battery under a very hot fire - placed our Battery to the left of his in an old field and opened fire. We fired 30 odd rounds apiece under a very hot fire from the enemies batteries which were only about 500 yards distant - They fired grape and cannister at us all together. We had no infantry to protect us, and the enemy's sharpshooters opened on us. Lieut (Hardin) tried to get a company to protect us, but could not, and we left our position."

---Cpl. John E. Magee, Stanford's Mississippi Battery, Stewart's Brigade

"Lieut. Hardin ... was the last to leave the position. ... As he was riding on after his guns a cannon ball passed entirely through his body. ... Some of the boys saw him fall and turned back to help him, but got to him in time to see him open his eyes and close them forever, without a struggle or a gasp."

---1st Sgt. William A. Brown, Stanford's Mississippi Battery, Stewart's Brigade

Night Moves

(Rosecrans and Bragg plan to attack each other's right flank Wednesday morning. But the Union commander moves slowly while Tuesday evening and into the night Bragg masses troops on his left flank for a surprise dawn attack:)

"We reached (Murfreesboro) ... the night before the battle began ..., crossing Stone's River on wagons standing in the water with boards reaching from one to another. It was a bitter cold night."

---John M. Berry, 8th Arkansas, Liddell's Brigade

"Our command was ordered to re-enforce the left wing, ... which we did by breaking the ice and wading Stone river. Several of our men were wounded that evening and night by the Yankee bombshells while lying in line upon the frozen ground without fires."

---Orderly Sgt. W.A. Garner, 25th Arkansas, McNair's Brigade

"When nightfall came (we) were in a lane with rail fences on each side, about four hundred yards from the main line of the enemy. Orders were to speak only in a whisper, as the enemy's pickets were not more than one hundred yards in front, the plan of battle being to take them by surprise next morning. We took down one of the lines of fence and spread the rails out over the ground next to the opposite string, which was left for breastworks. On the rails we passed the night without fires, most of the men sitting down watching the camp fires of the enemy some four hundred yards away, on an elevation. They were apparently ignorant of our being so close.

"We passed a most disagreeable night, having been on the battle field all of the night before and at times pelted with heavy showers during the (day). I fortunately had a good wool blanket that I had brought from home, one of the old-fashioned kind, with a hole in the middle large enough for a man's head. I stuck my head through, pulled my hat down, took my loaded gun under the banket, and thought of what would take place to-morrow."

---P.R. Jones, 10th Texas, Ector's Brigade

"Our brigade of McCown's Division (occupied) ... the extreme left. ... Company C (Kendrick's) spent the night in a large cornfield, the corn still on the stalk, with stacks of fodder here and there from which we drew bundles to rest upon as we listened all night long to the ... axes of the enemy, who were felling trees for breastworks. An all-night drizzle of rain added much to our discomfort."

---Joseph Hutcherson, 3rd Georgia Battalion, Rains' Brigade

(It is equally miserable for many Union outfits:)

"Our Regiment was ... in advance of all the others extending in line close behind a rail fence that divided the open field in front from the woods in the rear. Strict orders were issued that no fires should be allowed to disclose our position to the enemy. The air became quite cold after nightfall and we soon found it impossible to sleep. Some of my messmates with myself concluded to build a rail pen and line it with long dry grass from the field. ...

"One of my messmates, Sergeant Wertz, appeared to take no interest in our work but sat silently all through the night with his face buried in his hands. He gave no heed even when I threw my rubber blanket over his shoulders. ... Perhaps the shadow of impending fate darkened ... his mind. Before sunrise his bloody corpse laid amid the long dry grass in the field not twenty steps away from the rail pen where he sat through the night."

---Sgt. Maj. Widney, 34th Illinois, Kirk's Brigade

"We had marched about ten miles and laid in a cotton field with rain coming down on us all night without any fire to warm by. Some had their blankets, others including myself none, we pulled up the cotton bushes and laid them in the furrows for a bed and the water run under us all night."

---James G. Watson, 25th Illinois, Woodruff's Brigade

(Bragg shifts troops to the center of his line to be in position for the morning assault:)

"(Tuesday night) ... we were placed in line of battle on the north bank of Stone's River; and although the ground was frozen hard, we were not allowed a spark of fire. The Yankees were in line on the Wilkerson Pike with a battery composed of eighteen Napoleon guns, with their line of pickets and sharpshooters only three hundred yards in our front."

---S. Emory Sweet, 9th Tennessee, Maney's Brigade

"The night ... before the battle an incident took place such as history seldom records. The opposing lines ... were so near to each other as to be within easy bugle-call. ... Just before 'tattoo,' the military bands on each side began their evening music. The still winter night carried their strains to a great distance. At every pause on our side, far away could be heard the military bands of the other.

"Finally one of them struck up 'Home, Sweet Home.' As if by common consent, all other airs ceased, and the bands of both armies, far as the ear could reach, joined in the refrain."

---Samuel Seay, 1st Tennessee, Maney's Brigade

Dawn Attack

"On the eve of the battle of Murfreesboro, ... news reached Unionville (about 18 miles to the southwest) that General Bragg would attack ... early the next morning. In company with several friends, I decided to go and see the battle, as I had never been on a battlefield. Before sunrise ... (Wednesday) morning we were on the road."

---G.B. Moon, civilian

"Just before daybreak, General McNair brought his Arkansas brigade and placed it on our immediate right to fill up a gap, which appeared to complete all arrangements for the attack. ... Some whisky was passed down the line, of which more than half my company did not drink a drop, but others imbibed freely. It was ... given to the soldiers ... to warm them up after their long exposure to the rain and cold weather. Just about fairly good daylight, orders were given to move forward."

---Jones, 10th Texas, Ector's Brigade

"We were building fires and making coffee, for such permission had been granted just before daylight. One half of the (1st Ohio Light Artillery) Battery horses were unhitched and taken to the creek for water. ... The comfort of warming chilled fingers and toes and drinking a grateful cup of hot coffee outweighed for the moment any consideration of danger.

"Next, my curiosity asserted itself, and, while my comrades were still sipping their coffee, I leisurely walked out into the field towards the Picket line, where a company of our (regiment) was stationed to watch the enemy. Before reaching them I saw one running towards me, and as he passed me he exclaimed 'They're coming' and continued on to the Regiment to give the alarm. As all was so quiet, not a shot having been fired, I felt decidely skeptical and walked still further out until the enemy's breastworks were in view and there, sure enough, ... a succession of long lines of Gray were swarming over the Confederate breastworks and sweeping towards us but not yet within gun shot range.

"I started back in a hurry to rejoin the Regiment, and met it ... 350 men marching into an open field to meet 20,000. Our Regiment had advanced about 100 yards ... when our Pickets fired into the approaching columns of- the enemy."

---Sgt. Maj. Widney, 34th Illinois, Kirk's Brigade

"When we struck their skirmish line in the open field, we drove them back on their main line so rapidly that we got to within easy gunshot of their main line before they knew it."

---Lt. J.T. Tunnell, 14th Texas, Ector's Brigade

"Our weak challenge was answered with a volley from one of the advancing Regiments directly in front of us, and a moment later a succession of volleys spread to the right and left until the entire Confederate line was directing its fire into the ranks of our Regiment as we alone were visible to them. ...

"We threw ourselves flat in the grass and emptied 350 muskets into the ranks of the foe. ... Our Battery of six cannon opened a vigorous fire, throwing shells close over our heads into the enemy, whose Batteries also opened on us with shells and grape and cannister. ...

"Our only salvation was to lie flat as posssible on the ground, for the air fairly seethed with the 'Zip' of bullets and grape shot over out heads. It reminded me of the passage of a swarm of bees. ... Bullets ... plowed little furrows around us, throwing up tufts of grass and handsfull of soil into our faces or over our bodies, and others struck with a dull 'thud' into some poor unfortunate soul. ... (In) scarcely ten minutes ... 21 were killed and 100 wounded, or more than one third of our number. ... The Confederates were almost upon us. ... If our retreat had been delayed five minutes longer we could (not) have escaped. ...

"A piece of shell tore the heavy padded collar of my overcoat and ... spun me around and fairly choked me (and) ... made me think ... the missile had passed through my neck and that the choking ... was the symptom of a fatal wound. ... My delusion was so great that I could feel the blood flowing down my body, and I sat myself down to die. ... I was so sure of a gaping wound that I could not raise my hand to my neck until, as some moments elapsed and my strength did not appear to be ebbing away, I ventured to pass my hand around my neck and, to my great astonishment, found that it was only my coat collar that was shattered.

"I did not have much time to congratulate myself, for the charging columns of the enemy were ready to run over us. ... I have a vivid recollection of thrashing my way through a little patch of low scrubby (cedars) thickly strewn with rocks. All too low and small to afford any shelter but large enough to obstruct my progress while bullets were clipping the shrubs and glancing from rocks all around me."

---Sgt. Maj. Widney, 34th Illinois, Kirk's Brigade

"My regiment confronted a battery of six guns, ... but they fired only two or three shots ... until we were among them."

---Lt. Tunnell, 14th Texas, Ector's Brigade

"When I passed our Battery of six brass cannon their muzzles were still pointed to the foe, but they were silent and deserted, save by the dead and dying horses. Before I reached the Battery I saw the last Artilleryman cutting the traces of the last available horses galloping madly to the rear. ...

"In our retreat ... we encountered nothing but confusion until we reached the Nashville Turnpike."

---Sgt. Maj. Widney, 34th Illinois, Kirk's Brigade

"Many of the Yanks were either killed or retreated in their nightclothes. ... We found a caisson with the horses attached lodged against a tree and other evidences of their confusion. The Yanks tried to make a stand whenever they could find shelter of any kind. All along our route we captured prisoners, who would take refuge behind houses, fences, logs, cedar bushes and in ravines."

---Lt. Tunnell, 14th Texas, Ector's Brigade

"The boys ... (drove the enemy) back into their camps, which were well lit up with fires, around which they were cooking breakfast. Many were still in their 'pup' tents asleep and were killed while lying there. The onslaught was so sudden and the slaughter so great that they retreated in great confusion, every fellow for himself and the devil take the hindmost. ... They had abandoned everything ... to get away. ... One of their dead some two hundred yards to their rear ... had been killed still holding firmly to his pot of coffee."

---Jones, 10th Texas, Ector's Brigade

"While pursuing the fleeing Federals just back of a farm house near a clay hole and I think an old brick yard, ... (Capt. Thomas) remarked to me as I dropped on my knees to re-load, 'Come ahead old fellow we are driving them.' When I loaded and came up our command was reforming in great confusion. I then learned the Capt. had been killed in a few feet of where he had spoken to me. ... George Powell had taken his saber ... to save it for (Thomas' son) as (he) had requested the night before. It seems that he had a presentiment that he would be killed. Just before he made the fatal charge he remarked, 'Garner, I don't know how it is with you, but I have just had a strange dream about my wife and children and I feel that this is my last fight.' He had not more than finished the remark when order came, 'Forward march, charge bayonets.' "

---Sgt. Garner, 25th Arkansas, McNair's Brigade

"I ... ordered my battery to a gallop, and soon returned with it to the point where the Texans had captured the battery. ... I discovered ... on my right ... a large body of Federal infantry drawn up in line in front of the position, occupied by the captured guns and about 125 yards from my lead team. ...

"I was a little surprised at this but ordered the battery into position. ... I discovered that the enemy did not know whether I was friend or foe. ... As no time was to be lost, I ordered the gunners to commence firing with canister.

"The enemy doubtless hearing my command opened a break fire, wounding one man, and killing 3 horses and wounding three. ... The enemy's ranks ... stood but few discharges, when they retreated in considerable disorder."

---Capt. Douglas, Douglas' Texas Battery, Ector's Brigade

"As I sat on my horse in the grey dawn ... in the open field behind

Johnson's division, and saw it melting away before Hardee's yelling Confederates, I realized at once the critical position of our army. As ... ordnance officer of the right wing, I had charge of some seventy-six wagons, ... each drawn by four horses or mules. ...

"A single infantry company of about seventy-five men and two mounted orderlies had been assigned to me as train guards. ... I decided to direct my train toward the center of the infantry line, keeping well to the front. ...

"A detachment of Confederate cavalry charged wildly upon the train, attacking and endeavoring to stampede our teamsters and animals, but ... we repulsed the attack and moved on."

---Gates P. Thruston, McCook's ordnance officer

"Sixty-four of our number were captured after leaving the field by the enemy's cavalry, which had ridden around in our rear."

---Sgt. Maj. Widney, 34th Illinois, Kirk's Brigade

(Nearer the center of the Union line:)

"Securing a gun, but still barefoot, I started to find my regiment. ... Firing was ... heard down the pike. ... The firing ceased a moment and then opened with renewed vigor and from that time on it was nothing but the thunder of artillery, the crash of trees, as they splintered, the broken limbs falling to the ground and the boom of the shells as they burst overhead and all around. ...

"Just then there came a rush of men from the corn fields, soldiers from all regiments almost, some with guns and some without. I asked one of them what the matter was. 'The matter is we are most completely whipped,' says he. Just a moment after, a solid shot struck one of them, carrying away his leg.

"Just then the cavalry rode by, and ... one of them ... (said) to prevent being taken prisoner, I had better follow them. So I did, but it was hard work to walk barefoot over the icy ground ... and (I) ran great risk of being run over by wounded horses, that were dashing madly about with their harness dangling at their heels. Numbers of them were struck down around me. The balls hissed around so that it was a wonder to me I was not hit.

"Arriving at the wagons, the cavalry stopped and formed into line of battle. My feet paining me, for they were numb with cold, one of the teamsters told me to get into his wagon, which I did, just then an officer rode along and ordered the wagons to drive further down the line where they could be better protected but on starting they got into a panic. ... The ground was strewed with pots and kettles, pans, camp stoves, tents and boxes. ... They drove over guns, crushing them, every one of which cost Uncle Sam at least $20."

---Silsby, 24th Wisconsin, Sill's Brigade

"Wharton's cavalry ... charged over the fields in rear far down towards our infantry lines, sweeping everything. ... While in the open ... our ammunition train ... was discovered. ...

"I had already reported the importance of the train to every cavalry officer within reach, and appealed for protection. ... The 2d Ohio cavalry, ... the 4th Ohio cavalry, ... the 1st Ohio, the 2d East Tennessee and a battalion of the 3d Ohio cavalry were near at hand.

"Alas, when the crisis came ..., they were not in position to successfully withstand the shock. Wharton's ... artillery opened fire furiously on the Fourth Ohio Cavalry, and threw the regiment into some confusion. Soon apparently his entire command charged down upon us like a tempest, his troopers yelling like a lot of devils. They first struck the Fourth Ohio, which could make but little resistance. ...

"There was no staying the Confederates. They outnumbered and outflanked us, and to tell the melancholy truth, our defending cavalry ... left the ammunition train to its fate - high and dry in a corn field. ... Our teamsters, the train guards and the ordnance officer - yes, I must admit it - were not left far behind in the general stampede.

"We fired one volley from behind the protection of our wagons and then hunted cover in rear of a friendly fence and in the nearest thicket. Our teamsters outran the cavalry. Most of them never reappeared."

---Thruston, McCook's ordnance officer

"Our cavalry fled; closely following the wagons galloped the Texan Rangers, cheering and shouting to the teamsters to halt. Another moment and they were alongside the wagons, shooting (the teamsters) ... from the backs of their horses and mules.

"The driver of the wagon I was in fell dead from his horse. One of the butternuts seized hold of the horses' heads and stopped them. I jumped out and was taken prisoner. ... We were conveyed to the rear, and the teams started towards Murfreesboro. (A butternut) rode by with the Stars and Stripes on his shoulder, a handsome silk flag, with gold fringe."

---Silsby, 24th Wisconsin, Sill's Brigade

"The Confederates began to collect and lead away our teams and wagons and our condition seemed ... hopeless. ... Some of our cavalry rallied, other Union detachments came to the rescue. Wharton had soon to look to his own flanks, and was kept too busy to carry off our train."

---Thruston, McCook's ordnance officer

"The 4th Regular Cavalry came dashing down in hot pursuit of the Rebels, who, seeing they (were) about to lose their prisoners, commenced shooting them down. ... I started on the run towards our lines. ... One fellow fired his pistol at me twice but luckily missed. Another moment and our cavalry were up with us."

---Silsby, 24th Wisconsin, Sill's Brigade

"Six companies of the Fourth Regular Cavalry attacked Wharton's command. ... Soon two battalions of the Third Ohio Cavalry came up from the rear. ... (They) covered our front and held the enemy in check until our badly wrecked train, with its disabled wagons and scattered animals was reorganized and put in moving order. ...

"We were soon moving toward the Murfreesboro pike and the left of our army at double-quick speed. ... Just as we reached the Murfreesboro pike General Wheeler's (cavalry) troopers charged furiously upon escort and train and captured several wagons. ...

"We parked our long train ... near the Nashville pike and the lower ford of Stone's River. ... On our way, and at a critical time, we had been able to supply Gen. Phil Sheridan's retiring troops and others with ammunition. ... Nearly all the trains, supplies and baggage of the entire right wing had been captured or destroyed by the enemy's cavalry. ...

"We had saved the ordnance that was absolutely necessary to enable General Rosecrans to win the final victory."

---Thruston, McCook's ordnance officer

"I met a couple of men from the 24th Wis., I asked them where the Reg't was, they replied they did not know. I found two shoes, not mates, put them on, and proposed that we should go and find it. But they preferred staying where they were, so I started on alone. Shortly after I met a fellow from my own company, who told me that the Reg't was 'all cut to pieces, and what were not taken prisoners were scattered.' All I met sang the same tune, so I gave it up.

"Stopping at a spring near a hospital, every house for miles around was converted into one, a cavalry man told me that the Medical Director wanted to see me, so I went up to the house, where he told me he had the authority to take any person he came across and employ him as nurse in the hospital."

---Silsby, 24th Wisconsin, Sill's Brigade

(As the Union right collapses, Col. Philip S. Post of Gen. Davis' Division moves his brigade behind a fence and awaits the Rebel attack:)

"We was standing up in line when the enemy came out of the timber into the ... (corn) field; they was three or four lines deep. I could see the rebel officers riding behind their lines.

"There was no firing going on yet. The first order we got was to fix bayonets and then the command to march forward. ... The next order was to lie down; then we opened fire with every musket in the brigade. ... We had learned to shoot low.

"Our six splendid cannon poured volly after volly of grape and cannister shot into their ranks and mowed them down by swaths, but they closed their ranks.

"We lay there on the ground loading and firing as fast as we could ... for loading a muzzle loader and keeping very low down is hard to do. My hands was cold and numb and their bullets was coming pretty thick and fast. ... I looked up the corn row that I was on and saw the corn stalks clipped off with their bullets. ...

"In loading my gun ... I had to get up on my knees, and I thought to myself that I must not expose my sides so much for I did not want to be shot through the body. So I got down straight with my head down the corn row and thought to myself now, if you hit me, hit me in the head! ...

"It was not long until I discovered that I was hit, my hands and fingers was so cold I hardly knew when I was hit until I discovered the blood on both hands. ... I was hit twice and two bullets struck my gun in different places while it was in my hands.

"I still kept trying to shoot and the last shot I forgot to return my ramrod and sent that over to the rebels. ... That was not much of a misfortune to me, if I had happened to need a ramrod I could have easily gotten one, for we already had some men killed and wounded only a little ways from where I was and our guns was all alike, a fine Springfield Rifle and a good gun. ...

"Colonel P. Sidney Post ... saw the condition we was in and ordered one of his staff to go and tell us to fall back, but he was shot off his horse before he got near to us, and it was said that three commissioned officers lost their lives trying to get the order to us. ...

"Finally, there was a little fellow, a Private soldier that the Colonel had detailed for an orderly ... came in there and rode the full length of the troops. ... When he passed us, he said, 'Co. H, the Colonel thinks you had better fall back.' ...

"We got up and fell back slowly. We had to leave our dead and wounded. ... Some of the infantry had to help the battery boys pull their cannon by hand, they had not enough horses left."

---Alexander C. Pepper, 59th Illinois, Post's Brigade

(Close behind the retreating troops, Gen. St. John

Liddell's assault encounters little resistance until it runs into Col. Baldwin's reserve brigade near the Gresham house:)

"Passing through the yard of a nice farmhouse, we captured some of the Federal outposts, who pleaded for mercy. Gen. Liddell swore at them, telling them they were fine fellows, invading our country and then asking pardon. Old Jake, the bugler, whacked one of them over the head with his saber, saying, with an oath: 'You youst get home, den.'

"On we went, and in an open field we found ourselves face to face with the Federal force stationed behind a rail fence. I thought they would kill us all. We laid down ... and, firing as best we could, would roll over on our backs and load, then turn back and fire.

"I remember shooting right over Dick Jones's head. He looked back at me and said: 'John, you'll shoot me.' I said; 'No, I'll not. You keep your head down.' I loaded, and bang went my gun again, right at his ear. It so deafened and alarmed him that he turned again, used some very rough words, and declared I would kill him yet.

"Soon ... (McNair's) Texas brigade came up, swung into line, and charged the Federals. Those in our front gave way. ... We drove them across fields, through the woods, and into a cedar (hill). In the edge of some woods I came upon a wounded Federal. He had been shot in the knee. ... At his request I placed a piece of wood under his leg, so as to give him an easier position. I told him I was nearly dead for water. He offered me a drink from his canteen. ... I took a few swallows of the best water, it seemed, that I ever drank."

---Berry, 8th Arkansas, Liddell's Brigade

(By this time, G.B. Moon and his young sight-seeing companions have arrived to watch the battle:)

"Upon reaching the battlefield we were halted by guards, whom we flanked, and we pressed toward the smoke of battle. Near the edge of a small field, where many had fallen, I discovered a saber bayonet stuck up between two dead soldiers, one a Federal and the other a Confederate, lying close together, as if they had been placed in that position and marked with the bayonet for future recognition. I took the bayonet, ... though I have often regretted doing so. Both of these soldiers may have been lost to relatives by my thoughtlessness."

---Moon, civilian

(About 40 miles to the southeast of the battlefield, people in around McMinnville have been anxiously following the two armies' preliminary skirmishes. On the Old Shelbyville Road, just outside the Warren County seat, is Forest Home, residence of Col. John and Lucy Virginia French:)

"At daylight this morning very heavy cannonading was heard in the direction of Murfeesboro. It was a clear cold morning, with a brisk breeze setting from the North. I suppose there was 50 men left town for scene of conflict - and everything in the shape of a soldier went. Capt. Lawrence Butler and Andy Brown had an engagement to take tea with us this evening but as soon as the firing showed the ball to have opened in earnest, they sent an apology. ...

"All this morning there was a continuous roar of artillery - heaviest from 9 o'clock until noon. About 1 p.m. it was less frequent and seemed fainter."

---Virginia French

(At Beechwood, south of Murfreesboro, Katharine Cumming waits anxiously for word from her husband:)

"We were too far off to hear the firing of small arms. But O the booming of those cannon, the bursting of those shells. ... I received a number of communications direct from (my husband on) the field of battle during those days. ... They were scraps of soiled paper, minus envelopes, brought or sent by soldiers going to the rear, with just a few penciled lines; but O how I prized them!"

---Katharine Cumming

Hammering the Union Center

(Immediately to Post's left, Rebel brigades led by Sam Woods and Lucius Polk slam into Carlin's and Woodruff's brigades:)

"Their was a cornfield betwen us and the rebbels, and they had to run across that before they could reach us. ... Here came the rebels, yeling like indians."

---James K. Weir, 25th Illinois, Woodruff's Brigade

"We waited until they got near enough and then gave them a sudden volley which staggered them and they had to stop, but tried it again; as we were behind a fence, we had a little advantage of them and held them off for several charges. ...

"There was about the hardest fighting of the battle for three or four hours. We were driven from the fence three times, and twice took it again. ... Our battery, which was on our left, was supported by the 81st Indiana, but the enemy in the first grand rush captured one gun, but it was retaken by some of our company ('I') and Co. 'H', the rebels afterwards took it again, but it was finally retaken by Wood's Division."

---Watson, 25th Illinois, Woodruff's Brigade

"The rebbels ... had crosed over our (knapsacks) ... three times and had not disturbed them. By this time their was a great many kiled (and) wounded lying in the woods. Our Colonel was kiled also Daniel Dale and John Burley, our Captain, was shot in the arm.

"Wee had several wounded the last time wee run them off, and i did not think they would bother us agan, but wee saw the brigade on the right falen bach and the firing came nearer and directly it was one sheet of flame and smoke on our right. ...

"Wee had to run to save ourselves from being cut off. ... I had gave out in the runing and got behind the regt. The whole line of battle was runing for life.

"I thought everything was lost. I thought it was a stampede and a Manassas affair. The rebbels followed close and threw shot and shell at us till wee (got) into the timber, where our lines formed agan. Our division left the feild."

---Weir, 25th Illinois, Woodruff's Brigade

"The Rebels got the upper-hand over us and we had to retreat. I got a bullet through my thighs. ... I was left on the battlefield.

"The Rebels came around me from all sides. One cursed and said, 'Here lies a damn Yankee.' I lay still, but first they had to take some things from me. So they took my blanket, my canteen and a red-leather wallet that held all my letters from (my parents). Also they took a little case that contained needles and thread and other little things. They also took my 'Double Explanation' (of Catechism), and that I (missed) the most."

---Lars Olsen Dokken, 15th Wisconsin, Carlin's Brigade

(Maj. Gen. Jones M. Withers' division tries to smash the Union center and jam it against the shattered right wing. Only after he is reinforced by Maj. Gen. Frank Cheatham's division are the Yankees forced back:)

"The Federals (Woodruff's Brigade) were on a hill in the woods. ... (Withers') Alabamians had to go through an open field to attack. ... They were cut to pieces. ... The enemy cheered like a lot of little schoolboys."

---M'Dearman, 12th Tennessee, Vaughan's Brigade

"We were lying down until Withers gave way. ... Our men would guy and jeer the Alabamians for taking the back track as they passed through our line. One tall fellow said in reply to one of our boys, 'Yes, and you'll find it the hottest place that ever you struck in a little while.' His remark was about right."

---A.H. Brown, 13th Tennessee, Vaughan's Brigade

"Cheatham gave orders for every man ... at the command 'Attention' ... rise on his right knee and shoot under the smoke of the enemy's guns. Then we were to load and fire as we advanced. ... The enemy advanced downhill. We fired all at once, and rose yelling. ... When we got to where they were when we fired on them there was a blue line of dead Yanks across the field."

---M'Dearman, 12th Tennessee, Vaughan's Brigade

"Firing as we advanced, their first line waited until we got within easy range and then coolly delivered their fire; without waiting to reload they faced to the rear and double-quicked through their second line and reformed. ... The second line then awaited our approach, and though their men were falling fast around them, they cooly delivered their fire and retired through the first line and reformed. ... And thus they continued to fire and fall back until they were driven across a large field. Their lines were plainly marked by their dead, who lay thick upon the ground."

---Col. A.J. Vaughan, brigade commander

"We kept as close to them as possible, firing as we advanced. I saw a large ash tree in the edge of the woods, and made for it. When I reached it I was so nearly exhausted that I could scarcely get my breath. I took a swallow of water, and then reloaded my gun. Soon the Yanks' battery at our front in the woods opened on us with grape and canister, and then their infantry, too."

---M'Dearman, 12th Tennessee, Vaughan's Brigade

(Immediately to Vaughan's right, Maney's Brigade runs into Robert's Union brigade, supported by Houghtaling's and Hescock's batteries:)

"I was on the skirmish line. ... We were ordered forward to the attack. We were right upon the Yankee line on the (Wilkinson) ... turnpike."

---Sam R. Watkins, 1st Tennessee, Maney's Brigade

"Soon we ... found ourselves with the left four companies in a brick-yard, separated from the others by a pond perhaps thirty yards in width. Immediately in our front was the ... turnpike, well fenced on each side with high rail fences.

"I was deliberating upon the disadvantage of climbing them under fire, when, within less than two hundred yards of us, sharply diagonal to our right, came a volley of grape, canister, and shell, from a battery perfectly masked in a natural cedar brake. The men in the left wing instantly laid down in the brick-yard. ... The fire with some musketry was simply furious. ...

"The direction from which it came impressed the minds of the men with the belief that it was our own friends who did the shooting."

---Seay, 1st Tennessee, Maney's Brigade

"The Yankees were shooting down our men by scores. A universal cry was raised, 'You are firing on your own men.' (But) the whole skirmish line halloowed, and kept on telling them that they were Yankees, and to shoot; but the order was to cease firing. ... We were not twenty yards from the Yankees, and they were pouring the hot shot and shells right into our ranks; and every man was yelling at the top of his voice, 'Cease firing, you are firing on your own men; cease firing, you are firing on your own men.' "

---Watkins, 1st Tennessee, Maney's Brigade

"Lieutenant James, then serving as staff-officer, ... was so thoroughly convinced that this was the case that he lost his life in a gallant attempt to stop it by riding up to the battery. Captain Thomas H. Malone ... was, at his own request, sent around our right to ... a point within some thirty yards of the battery, and ascertained the number of their pieces, their position, and the fact that it was the enemy. His horse was wounded, and his clothes received several bullets, but he escaped unhurt.

"It was not until after his return, when a considerable time had elapsed - Turner's splendid battery, armed with Napoleon guns, captured at Perryville, Kentucky, by the First Tennessee, having opened in our rear, and Colonel Feild's ... command having been given to 'Fire on that battery, anyhow' - that the regiment began an irregular reply."

---Seay, 1st Tennessee, Maney's Brigade

"Oakley, color-bearer of the Fourth Tennessee Regiment, ran right up in the midst of the Yankee line with his colors, begging his men to follow. I hallooed until I was hoarse, 'They are Yankees, they are Yankees; shoot, they are Yankees.' ... The crest occupied by the Yankees was belching ... fire and smoke, and the Rebels were falling like leaves of autumn in a hurricane. ... They fell back and re-formed."

---Watkins, 1st Tennessee, Maney's Brigade

"The brigade to our right made a vigorous assault. The necessity of meeting these new-comers caused the Federals to withdraw their fire in great measure from us."

---Seay, 1st Tennessee, Maney's Brigade

"General Cheatham came up and advanced. I did not fall back, but continued to load and shoot until a fragment of a shell struck me on the arm, and then a minnie ball passed through the same (arm), paralyzing my arm. ... I grabbed my arm. I thought it had been torn from my shoulder. ...

"The brigade had fallen back about two hundred yards. ... General Cheatham ... was calling on the men ..., 'Come on, boys, and follow me.' ... I felt sorry for him, he seemed so earnest and concerned, and as he was passing me I said, 'Well, General, if you are determined to die, I'll die with you.'

"We were ... at least a hundred yards in advance of the brigade, Cheatham all the time calling upon the men to come on. He was leading the charge in person."

---Watkins, 1st Tennessee, Maney's Brigade

"Promptly at the first lull, ... our colonel (shouted) 'Forward, First Tennessee infantry!' Every man, with gun loaded and cocked, cartridge box open ... instantly sprang forward. The fences that had disturbed (my) imagination were no longer there. That furious cannonade had left no rail upon another.

"As we crossed the pike into the open field beyond, the Federal battery ... was endeavering to escape over a road cut through the cedars. A gallant brigade of infantry which had been its support, in the most perfect order, and with hardly an attempt to return our fire, emerged from the cedars and was double-quicking diagonally across our front."

---Seay, 1st Tennessee, Maney's Brigade

"Maney's brigade raised a whoop and yell, and swooped down on those Yankees like a whirl-a-gust of woodpeckers in a hail storm, paying the blue coated rascals back. ... Every man's gun was loaded, and ... when they did fire, there was a sudden lull in the storm of battle. ... With cheers and shouts they charged up the hill, shooting down and bayoneting the flying cannoneers, General Cheatham, Colonel (Hume) Feild and (Capt.) Joe Lee slashing with their swords."

---Watkins, 1st Tennessee, Maney's Brigade

"Our officers hallooed: 'Charge, men! charge! ... We raised a yell,

sent a volley into their lines, started at them and never stopped until we got the battery of six guns. Then our command turned some of those guns upon them."

---M'Dearman, 12th Tennessee, Vaughan's Brigade

"As we came into full view, with no obstructions between us, the long deferred fire from the Confederates became terrific. ... The work at this point was short and rapid, and the Confederate fire cool and deliberate. In what appeared to be but a few minutes no foe remained in sight. ... Stretched before and behind us, in every crevice in the rocks, ... the Federal wounded had crept for shelter. Mangled masses of human forms, torn in every conceivable way, lay scattered in all directions. ...

"The rectified alignment threw (me) well past the right four pieces of the Federal battery, which stood perhaps fifteen paces in our front. Of the horses which drew these six pieces and their caissons not one was on his feet. Most were dead, and all the rest wounded. When the command 'Forward,' was given, (I) passed between two pieces and two caissons, the twelve horses and six riders to which - the latter with whips still clinched in their hands - lay dead on each side."

---Seay, 1st Tennessee, Maney's Brigade

"I cannot remember now of ever seeing more dead men and horses and captured cannon all jumbled together, than that scene of blood and carnage ... on the (Wilkinson) ... Turnpike; the ground was literally covered with blue coats dead."

---Watkins, 1st Tennessee, Maney's Brigade

(Withers' division resumes its pressure on the Yankee center, near battlefield tour Stop 4:)

"Our regiment was on ... a large field in which corn had grown, but the stalks had been cut. ... The Yankees had planted a battery in the cedar grove across the field, and the 29th and 30th Mississippi regiments were ordered to charge and take the battery. ... When we started across the field ... I thought those were the deepest middles between corn rows that I had ever seen. The Yanks held their fire until we were within thirty yards of them; they ... then opened fire. ... They were among the trees, while we were in an open field, so they were just mowing us down like weeds."

---J.E. Robuck, 29th Mississippi, P. Anderson's Brigade

"A cornfield was in front of the 21st Ohio, and as soon as the rebels came in range, the infantry opened a deadly fire on them. ... Men fell at every step, and still they pressed forward. 'Cap, do you want to see that man come out of that saddle?' 'Yes' - and the horse was without a rider. 'Gosh! I had a dead one on him' 'He'll never kill any more Yanks.' Such are some of the expressions made by the men."

---Capt. S.S. Canfield, 21st Ohio, Miller's Brigade

"We were ordered to fall down ... to escape their bullets, shells and cannon balls. ... I changed my opinion about the middles - they appeared to be entirely too shallow."

---Robuck, 29th Mississippi, P. Anderson's Brigade

"When the enemy was only about thirty yards distant, the order was given to 'fix bayonets;' but about this time they broke and fled."

---Capt. Canfield, 21st Ohio, Miller's Brigade

"We were ... ordered to retreat, which we did in double quick across the field, while thousands of Yankee bullets and cannon balls whistled close to our ears."

---Robuck, 29th Mississippi, P. Anderson's Brigade

"Shortly after the repulse, Lieutenant Colonel Neibling came along the regiment and said, 'My God boys! we gave 'em Hell; didn't we?' "

---Capt. Canfield, 21st Ohio, Miller's Brigade

"The remainder of the two brigades were again formed into line ... (and) ordered to take the Yankee batteries, which it did. ... I soon got a little 'scratch' and was detailed, with Pat Rankin, to take three hundred prisoners to the rear and guard them."

---Robuck, 29th Mississippi, P. Anderson's Brigade

"The enemy ... passed us on both flanks (and Col. Neibling) ... called out, 'Fall back, we are surrounded!' "

---Capt. Canfield, 21st Ohio, Miller's Brigade

"One of the last sights witnessed as we entered the cedar woods in our retreat was an artilleryman trying to haul his gun off the field with one horse, the other five having been killed. One wheel of the gun carriage had become fastened between two rocks, and the brave artilleryman was trying with a rail to pry it out. What became of him, I know not, but we lost five out of the nine pieces of artillery with which we began the battle."

---Gibson, 78th Pennsylvania, Miller's Brigade

"How we got back through the cedars I can never tell, except that we walked - we didn't run. ... The men ... became badly scattered, and mixed with other commands, but a portion of them was collected, who procured ammunition and took position in support of the Board of Trade Battery, near the (Nashville) pike."

---Capt. Canfield, 21st Ohio, Miller's Brigade

"My regiment was standing in double columns massed on the two center companies on the reserve line, waiting orders, (when) a staff officer from General George H. Thomas' head-quarters in the field rode up to me and said, hurriedly: 'Colonel, I have orders for you. The regiment on your front has been nearly annihilated. Hold your men in hand while I go on the line and clear off what is left; and you watch me, and when ready, I will wave my sword three times for you; and do you come on, advancing on the line of battle firing,' and off he went.

"I turned to my regiment, and said: 'Comrades, we go into action in a few minutes. Off caps, and say your prayers!'

"Whilst we were all praying, I watched as well as prayed. Presently the sign was given, and I interrupted their devotions with 'Battalion, attention! Order arms! shoulder arms! right shoulder arms! forward, quick time, march!'

"Approaching the battle-line, I gave the order: 'Battalion, by right and left companies, outward face; by right and left half wheel, forward into line, advance firing; march!' ...

"I was wounded in the calf of my right leg. A ball tore through the clothing of my left leg at the knee.

"Being ordered to advance on the foe firing, I changed the position of my pistol from its position at my right shoulder, and suspended it over my right breast, so as to have it handy at my front. ... A bullet or bullets struck me in my right breast with awful force, and nearly unseated me from my saddle. I put my hand to my breast, which was writhing with a stinging sensation, and found that my pistol was shattered by the shots; the ramrod was broken off, and the handle, some five inches to the right, was shattered in fragments. ...

"My horse was shot under me; three balls entering him at once. ... One ball struck his lower jaw, just where his bridle-bits work; one ball struck him in the shoulder, about two inches from the bend of my knee. One ball struck him two inches back of the root of his ear. ... The dead and wounded and dying were in every direction. It was indeed a storm of death."

---Col. Granville Moody, 74th Ohio commander, Miller's Brigade

"I was wounded just above the left knee, by a musket-ball or a piece of shell ... and taken to the field hospital, five miles toward

Nashville."

---Owens, 74th Ohio, Miller's Brigade

"My regiment was discomfited and scattered. I was endeavoring to rally them. As I went over a vacant field I overtook six of my men with a first lieutenant fleeing toward Nashville. I cried out: 'Hello, men, there is your regiment to the left. Rally to your regiment!' But they were intent on escape, and kept right on. I rode past and turned, facing them, and presenting my pistol, cried: 'Halt!' I threatened a pistol-ball to the man that took another step toward Nashville.

"The officer said: 'Colonel, we are dazed, and don't know what we are doing. If we will at once return to duty, will you report us?' I instantly lowered my pistol and assured them that no man should hear from me. The lieutenant shouted: 'Three cheers for Colonel Moody!' They were given, and the men joined their regiment.

"I rode on in search of further squads, and as I neared a wooded region, a company of nine or ten 'gray-backs' sprange out of the woods and opened fire upon me. Soon six more joined them and commenced firing. My horse was soon crippled, stopped short and stood still. I applied the spurs, he trembled and shrunk, and fell in agony to the ground, dead. I disentangled myself from him, dislodged my two pistols from the holsters, and began my retreat from the men who were firing at me. But in the morning I had received a bullet wound in my right leg below the knee, and I had to limp away from the firing of ten or twelve men.

"Just as the firing became rapid, and the bullets were singing wildly around my head and person, a horseman rushed up between me and those firing upon me, and dismounting from his steed shouted: 'Here Colonel, get into the saddle and get away quick.' ... A rebel colonel (had been shot) ... from his horse, which ran wildly, with the empty saddle, and Patrick (name for any unidentified Irish soldier) had caught him, and mounting, rode down to me in a gallop, just in time to save me. ...

"I attempted to mount the horse, but failed. My right leg that was wounded was so stiff that it would not straighten out to the stirrup by about three inches. I said, 'Comrade, get into the saddle yourself, and let me take my chances.' (He replied,) 'Divil a bit; try again, Colonel. Try again, man, or the divils will get you, sure.' I tried again, and Patrick almost lifted me into the saddle, and amidst the 'zipping' bullets, which came thick and fast, I strode the saddle, and without waiting to find the stirrups I started for our lines. Patrick nearly kept pace with my frenzied, flying steed, and as we approached our line of men, they ... shouted: 'Hurrah! Bravo! Colonel, are you hit anywhere?' ...

"Poor Patrick was killed ... in the engagement that followed. ... I received a severe shot through the breast of my coat, grazing and glancing along my breast. ... My clothes were pierced with holes, though not a ball touched my person on this occasion. My coat-front was torn as if a tiger had clawed me. It was on account of this and at this time that my regiment nicknamed me the 'Ragged Colonel.' ... I ... lost three horses, and my fine overcoat that cost me sixty dollars."

---Col. Moody, 74th Ohio commander, Miller's Brigade

(As the Rebel brigades press on, their wounded and prisoners stream to the rear:)

"As I walked to the field hospital, I overtook another man walking along. ... His left arm was entirely gone. His face was as white as a sheet. The breast and sleeve of his coat had been torn away, and I could see the frazzled end off his shirt sleeve, which appeared to be sucked into the wound.

"I looked at it pretty close, and I said, 'Great God!' for I could see his heart throb, and the respiration of his lungs. ... All at once he dropped down and died without a struggle or a groan. ...

"In passing over the battle-field, I came across a dead Yankee Colonel. He had on the finest clothes I ever saw, a red sash and fine sword. I particularly noticed his boots. I needed them, and had made up my mind to wear them out for him. ... I took hold of the foot and raised it up and made one trial at the boot to get it off. I happened to look up, and the Colonel had his eyes wide open, and seemed to be looking at me. He was stone dead, but I dropped that foot quick. It was my first and last attempt to rob a dead Yankee."

---Watkins, 1st Tennessee, Maney's Brigade

"When Pat and I had succeeded in landing our three hundred Yankees safely in the rear, far beyond the reach or range of bullets, we met Joe Coward, who still held to his gun. So I asked if he was lost. I knew that Joe had fought in the first two charges made on the enemy. ... His only reply to my question was a quotation, 'He who fights and runs away, May live to fight another day. ...' "

---Robuck, 29th Mississippi, P. Anderson's Brigade

"General Hardee directed me to parole all prisoners that were not dangerously wounded at a large Federal field hospital on the Wilkinson Pike, located in and around the Griscom House, that had been swept over by the Confederate lines. ...

"In the house upstairs and downstairs, in outhouses, and on the grass surrounding the house. ... the inspector general of the army ... reported ... about six hundred officers and men. These ... were ... from the slightly wounded, who were usually cheerful and talkative, to the mortally wounded. ...

"The Federal litter bearers brought in the body of an officer, which was laid on the grass outside the house, clothed in a somewhat worn undress uniform without insignia of rank. He was of slight build, rather thin-visaged face, full sandy whiskers. The wound was from a Minie ball just below the cheek bone, the blood from which had slightly flowed down on his whiskers. ...

"It was the body of (U.S) Brig. Gen. Joshua Sill."

---Col. W.D. Pickett, assistant inspector general

Rosecrans' Last Ditch

(While Rosecrans hustles reserves, artillery and retreating units into a last-ditch line along the Nashville Pike, Rebel brigades regroup for another push against the battered Yankee right wing:)

"We had by this time become badly scattered, ... keeping up a running fight for two and one-half miles. ... I fell in with Adjutant Sparks of my regiment soon after we became scattered, and, coming to a log pen in a cotton patch that appeared to have about sufficient seed cotton in it to make two bales, noticed that the top of the pile had been lately disturbed. ... Sparks picked up a stick ... and remarked: 'I will just strike a match and set this cotton on fire.' With this, he scratched his stick across the door, when lo and behold, eight Yankees jumped out of the cotton and raised their hands. ...

"By this time quite a number of our men overtook us and joined in the pursuit. We turned our prisoners over to some of our men, who carried them to the rear. We continued in pursuit quite a distance from the cotton pen and ran up on a line of the enemy that looked like a brigade lying down on the crest of a ridge, doubtless expecting our men to run on them and be taken by surprise.

"But in this they were mistaken, for, while only their heads were visible, we took the drop on them by firing first, killing about half, the rest jumping up and running at full speed to their rear and disappearing in a dense cedar brake."

---Jones, 10th Texas, Ector's Brigade

"We drove them helter-skelter ... about three miles, when we halted to reform ... at the south side of a small open field, beyond which was a heavy grove of timber, mostly red cedar, into which the enemy had retreated. ... We sent forward a line of skirmishers and then followed in line of battle. We encountered the enemy at the edge of the cedar brake."

---Lt. Tunnell, 14th Texas, Ector's Brigade

"On the extreme right of the brigade ... Capt. Meredith Kendrick had been disabled from a severe wound in the thigh, lying with his head against a tree, pale from the loss of blood. W.D. Clark, a private in Company C, ... went to him, offering to help him to the rear, but he declined. ... Private Clark, then looking toward the enemy ... was struck in the jugular vein and fell dead at Captain Kendrick's feet. Within a few feet (I) ... was wounded in the left arm."

---Hutcherson, 3rd Georgia Battalion, Rains' Brigade

(To the Rebels' right, General Rousseau's division moves

into the cedar forest to delay the Confederate attack. Brigades commanded by Col. John Beatty, Col. Benjamin Scribner and Col. Oliver Shepherd take position. At Stop 3 on the battlefield tour:)

"General Rousseau points me to the place he desires me to defend and enjoins me to 'hold it until hell freezes over,' at the same time telling me that he may be found immediately on the left of my brigade with Loomis' battery. ... An open wood is in my front; but where the line is formed, and to the right and left, the cedar thicket is so dense ... it (is) impossible to see the length of a regiment.

"The enemy (Rains' Brigade) comes up directly and the fight begins. ... My men are ... concealed by the cedars, while the enemy, advancing through the open woods, is fully exposed. ... The Third Ohio, the Eighty-eighth and Forty-second Indiana hold the position and deliver their fire so effectively that the enemy is finally forced back. ...

"The enemy (brigades under Polk and Wood) makes another and more furious assault on my line. After a fierce struggle, lasting from forty to sixty minutes, we succeed in repelling this also. I send ... to General Rousseau, and am soon informed that neither he nor Loomis' battery can be found.

"Troops are reported to be falling back hastily, and in disorder, on my left. I ... ascertain that Scribner's and Shepherd's brigades are gone. I conclude that ... hell has frozen over, ... about face my brigade and march to the rear. ...

"Not far from the Murfreesboro pike, I find the new line of battle and take position. Five minutes after, the enemy strike us. ... The regiments on our left get into disorder and finally become panic-stricken. The fright spreads, and my brigade sweeps by me to the open field in our rear.

"I hasten to the colors, stop them, and endeavor to rally the men. The field is ... covered with flying troops. ... My brigade, however, begins to steady itself on the colors, when my horse is shot under me and I fall heavily to the ground. ... My troops, with thousands of others, sweep in disorder to the rear, and I am left standing alone."

---Col. J. Beatty, 3rd Ohio, brigade commander

(The Rebel attack pushes closer to Rosecrans' final line at the Nashville Pike:)

"Away to the right the noise of the combat was growing louder, more distinct, more small arms firing, every thing showing it was a big fight. Across the cotton-fields a few men straggled leisurely to the rear; an ambulance trotted out of the cedars with wounded men, then a squad of soldiers moved rather briskly away from the front;

"I saw the number of sound men growing larger very rapidly; it looked badly, as the crowd increased every moment. ... I was mortified to see a color guard with their regimental flags falling back, and then the swarm grew apace, so that I thought I was in the midst of another Bull Run. ... Hundreds of men and officers, mingled with cannons, ambulances, and what not, (were) hurrying out of the cedars toward the turnpike to Nashville.

"A battery walking their horses, and at regular intervals, caught my eyes as they debouched from the cedars right in front of me, which I recognized as the First Michigan, (also known as Loomis' Battery) under the command of First Lieutenant Van Pelt. ... At the same moment General Rousseau, followed by a single orderly, advanced at a gallop from the cedars. I spurred my horse toward him. ... I said, 'General, shall I post the battery where my (ammunition) wagons are? It is the best position on the field.'

" 'Do it instantly. Tell Van Pelt I will get him infantry support,' and away he went to look for troops. I galloped over the cotton patch and delivered my order to Lieutenant Van Pelt, who was as cool as if on a march. He looked at the spot I pointed out, nodded ... and rode away to direct the foremost piece of the battery.

"Then I put my horse at full speed, reached my wagons, and moved them into the slight depression behind the knoll they had stood upon, parked them as closely as possible, dismounted all the drivers, telling them to lie down under the wagons and keep as quiet as they could. ... The fields around had become covered with troops much demoralized and mingled in ... confusion."

---Alfred Pirtle, 1st Michigan Artillery

"Going back to the railroad, I find my men, General Rousseau, Loomis, and, in fact, the larger part of the army. The artillery has been concentrated at this point and now opens on the advancing columns of the enemy."

---Col. J. Beatty, 3rd Ohio, brigade commander

"Lieutenant Van Pelt had opened fire, drawing some return from the infantry in the edges of the woods; another battery had been posted directly to his right, and was firing occasionally. ...

"There came a lull in the noises of the battle. ... I was standing near a gun ... to the rear of the First Michigan battery, looking at the dark cedars where I knew the enemy were. ... In front of us was a small space ... then the turnpike, then the cotton patch about three hundred yards wide. Toward the right of this cotton patch was a clump of bushes, tall weeds, and dried grass. Lying about the surface of the cotton patch were some dead men, and some wounded men in gray moving now and then, but not much;

"No signs of life in the cedars, but all eyes were fixed there, for in their depths the enemy had gone, and from them they must come or into them we must go."

---Pirtle, 1st Michigan Artillery

"The cedars were very dense, making it difficult to keep an alignment while going through to open ground on the opposite side.

"Those who got through were met with such a volley of grape and canister from about forty cannon that had been hurriedly placed there ... that they beat a retreat through the dense cedars as best they could."

---Jones, 10th Texas, Ector's Brigade

"As I looked, a man on foot, sword in hand, with a shout (dashed) into view; the edge of the timber was in an instant alive with a mass of arms, heads, legs, guns, swords, gray coats, brown coats, shirt sleeves, and the enemy were upon us - yelling, leaping, running! Not a shot from them for a few jumps; then one or two paused to throw up their pieces, fire and yell, then run forward. ...

"Our two batteries together fired, covering the field with a cloud of smoke, hiding every object in it. ... As fast as they could load, they fired into the cloud. They ceased, and not a moving object was in front. ...

"The dead and wounded had been dreadfully increased, while cries and groans reached our ears. On our side, men and horses had been killed and wounded, yet no large loss was inflicted. One of the Michigan men lay almost at my feet, wounded badly, but refused to leave the spot. ...

"I felt sure the enemy would make another charge. ... I heard (Major Loomis, chief of artillery in Rousseau's Division) ... tell Van Pelt the enemy was going to make another charge, and 'You give them double-shotted canister as hot as hell will let you.' He went over to the Regular battery, where Lieutenant Fred Guenther and his second Lieutenant, Israel Ludlow, were preparing for the next charge, and gave them the same ... orders. ... The guns (were) ... depressed ... to rake the ground from the turnpike to the cedars. ...

"The enemy were reconnoitering the position carefully, keeping out of sight as much as possible, though now and then one would be seen, yet the silence was ominous. Our army was moving into a new position, making the batteries the pivot or center."

---Pirtle, 1st Michigan Artillery

"The Confederates uncovered from the cedar woods by three distinct lines visible for the charge."

---Capt. S.F. Horrall, 42nd Indiana, J. Beatty's Brigade

"These lines ... advanced across the open rapidly and completely uncovered, and then our batteries opened on them a deafening unceasing fire, throwing twenty-four pounds of iron from each piece, across that small space. ... I never saw guns served as fast. ... Before the recoil was expended the gunners grasped the spokes and threw the pieces into position; ... the swab was run in, the handle turned, withdrawn, the charge sent home, and the gun fired.

"Such a roar was deafening. ... The enemy ... were swarming across the field, firing and shouting. ... We could get sight now and then of their waving arms and guns, while every few seconds a bullet would hiss near us or we would see some man fall, or perhaps, a horse rear, plunge, and drop. ... The charge (kept) ... coming, coming on like the ... sea, ever nearer at each succeeding wave.

"But men were not born who could longer face that storm of canister. ... They broke, they fled, and some took refuge in the clump of trees and weeds I mentioned."

---Pirtle, 1st Michigan Artillery

"George Powell and hundreds of others were killed there. It was our time to run. I was wounded and ordered to the rear."

---Sgt. Garner, 25th Arkansas, McNair's Brigade

"The artillery opened on us and cut the timber off over our heads, and it seemed that the heavens and the earth were coming together. Our men sheltered themselves as best they could behind trees, ledges of rocks. ... Their front line of battle ... seemed to take fresh courage and began to advance upon us, walking a few steps, then firing and falling down to load. ...

"We having only one line and the men badly scattered, I began to look around for a superior officer to advise with. ... I saw Colonel Andrews, of the 32nd Texas of our brigade, coming down the line from the right, running from one large tree to another waving his hand to the rear. ... So, we retreated out of the cedars and across the open field, where we again reformed our lines."

---Lt. Tunnell, 14th Texas, Ector's Brigade

"Those of us who got back to an opening were greatly demoralized. ... Littleton Fowler, who once preached at Jacksonville, took refuge among the cedars behind some rocks and said that the cannonading was so terrific he could have caught birds that were so benumbed they could not fly. General McCown and his staff finally persuaded the men from every regiment in that part of the army to line up regardless of company or regiment and be ready for an attack."

---Jones, 10th Texas, Ector's Brigade

"Our shouts ... were taken up right and left, as soon as it was seen that the charge had been repulsed, while hand-shaking and congratulations were going on at every side, which ... changed to a perfect frenzy of cheers when an officer rode out from our lines and returned with a group of prisoners."

---Pirtle, 1st Michigan Artillery

"Under the smoke and underbrush forty or fifty Confederate privates, throwing down their arms, crawled on hands and knees, surrendering as prisoners of war. ... A more forlorn, worn-out, and famished set of men would be hard to find. ... They were turned over to (me) ..., whose duty as brigade inspector it was to turn them over to the provost marshal. I said: 'Boys, you are worn and hungry?' 'Yes, on duty fighting or otherwise twenty-four hours, with little to eat.' 'Well, you must be fed,' I replied. So, marching to commissary headquarters, they were fed."

---Capt. Horrall, 42nd Indiana, J. Beatty's Brigade

"After General Ector got his men together we were moved up on our right and took position ... close ... to the enemy, who appeared reluctant to renew the battle, though at times they would send over some cannon balls to remind us they were in our front."

---Jones, 10th Texas, Ector's Brigade

The Deadly Forest

(As the Union's right wing and center give way, Gen. James R. Chalmers' Mississippi Brigade charges the cedar woods where the Union line crosses the Nashville & Chattanooga Railroad track. Survivors on both sides quickly dub it "Hell's Half-Acre" and "The Slaughter Pen." The spot, Stop 8 on the Stones River park tour, is better known as "The Round Forest":)

"At 10 the reg(imen)t opened on the enemy which were advancing upon us at double quick. They were drawn up in three lines. ... The first line was brought to a sudden halt ... within 200 yards of our reg(imen)t by the terrific fire from our men and 2 batteries ... one on our right and one on our left."

---Capt. E.S. Holloway, 41st Ohio, Hazen's Brigade

"Then commenced the most terrible cannonading I ever witnessed, our one hundred canon were belching forth their deadly contents at once, while thousands of small arms kept up a roar equal to the falls of Niagara. Men were swept down by hundreds - trees shrubs and everything was torn up cut off or shivered. ... Our battery took 4 different positions, all of which we suffered a loss in. For over an hour this deadly conflict was kept. ...

"Wm. C. Brooks, was shot down by a canon ball while acting No. 1 at the gun. I was no. 2 and within 6 inches of him when he was struck. His last words were, looking me straight in the face 'Oh Lord, I'm killed.' ... Richard Y. Elliott was killed by the same ball at his post No. 3. He was perfectly unconscious what hurt him."

---Cpl. Magee, Stanford's Mississippi Battery, Stewart's Brigade

"Elliott having the lower part of his face torn away causing instant death. Brooks shot through the body as he was ... ramming a shot down the gun. He fell dead almost instantly."

---1st Sgt. Brown, Stanford's Mississippi Battery, Stewart's Brigade

"I was struck with a spent ball in the breast and knocked down but it only lasted for a few seconds before I was again on my feet. It caused a slight bruis. Had it had a little more force it would have made shure work. ...

"We held this position for 40 minutes when we were relieved by the 9th Indiana Reg(imen)t our ammunition being exhausted. The men having fired 60 rounds each."

---Capt. Holloway, 41st Ohio, Hazen's Brigade

(Chalmers' battered brigade flees from the Round Forest's fierce defensive fire, but Donelson's Tennessee Brigade swarms around the charred remains of the Cowan house and drives Cruft's Brigade from the edge of the woods. However, reinforcements and artillery support help Col. William B. Hazen's Brigade hold onto the Round Forest. Bragg orders Breckinridge's division to cross Stones River and storm the position. Adam's and Jackson's brigades arrive first. Instead of waiting for the division to assemble, Gen. Leonidas Polk hurls the two brigades against the Round Forest:)

"Though a non-combatant, I was with my regiment during the entire battle, comforting the dying, carrying off the wounded and caring for them. ... Our position was between Stone River on our left and the railroad and turnpike on our right, and directly in front of Breckenridge's Corps. ... Our regiment ... three times charged ... (Adam's) Brigade and three times put the enemy to flight. ...

"Of my own regiment every alternate man was either killed or wounded. ... Captain Templeton fell, fatally wounded. I carried him to the rear and remained at his side, until he breathed his last. I copied his last message and sent it to his friends at home. My own next-door neighbor in Westville, Ind., Captain J.N. Foster, dropped mortally wounded into my arms, the same ball killing two other brave soldiers.

"Colonel I.C.B. Suman, of the Ninth Indiana, was shot twice, one ball severing the artery in the arm, the other penetrating the body and lodging between two ribs, whence I pulled it out. One boot was filled with blood and he was bleeding his life away."

---Rev. John M. Whitehead, 15th Indiana, Wagner's Brigade

"When Chaplain Whitehead gave me his assistance, he was all besmeared with the blood of the wounded he had cared for."

---Col. I.C.B. Suman, 9th Indiana, Hazen's Brigade

"I dressed ... (Col. Suman's) wounds and helped him on his horse and he rode back into the raging battle.

"John Long, a private, had one leg shot to pieces. He cut the dangling limb off with his pocketknife and hobbled off using his gun for a crutch, until I took him up and carried him to the rear.

"Calvin Zenner of Company G, received a fatal wound. I carried him back. A number of soldiers gathered around the dying comrade, and I offered a prayer for him. He talked to all of us and then said: 'Now boys, let us all once more sing a song together.' And he struck up the hymn, 'O Sing to Me of Heaven.' Then he said: 'Good-bye boys, I am going home. I am mustered out.' And he closed his eyes and ceased to breathe."

---Rev. Whitehead, 15th Indiana, Wagner's Brigade

"Through a shower of grape, shell and canister ... (we) worked steadily across an open field, while men were falling at every step.

Soon we reached the place now known as the Slaughter Pen, when both sides turned loose with their rifles. ...

"Our single brigade contended against four brigades of the Yankees and seventeen pieces of artillery. ... We charged in fifty yards of them and had not the timely order of retreat been given - none of us would now be left to tell the tale. ... Our regiment carried two hundred and eighty into action and came out with fifty eight. ...

"One ball struck my sword, another passed through my coat collar and another through the leg of my boot."

---J. Morgan Smith, 32nd Alabama, Adams' Brigade

(As Adams' and Jackson's brigades stagger back, Breckinridge arrives with his two remaining brigades, under Preston and Palmer. Their attack is also hindered by the Cowan house out-buildings and fences:)

"At (1:30) p.m. the ... roar of musketry is as regular and quick as touching the two lowest keys on the piano. We stood about 1/2 an hour listening when our aide rode up to Gen. Preston. ... We were ordered to load. ...

"(About 2:30) p.m. ... we double quicked back through the field and waded Stone River, wetting us up to our knees, and formed in line of battle just on the west side of the creek, or river. We had thrown off our blankets ... before crossing. ...

"At the creek, ambulances were crossing with the wounded; one man walking with his arm shot off enquired what (regiment) ... as our beautiful flag passed him, and being told the 4th Fla. said, 'You'll do it up right; pay them for my arm.' A little soldier ... was in one of the ambulances and appeared to be hit in four or five places. His back, I think, was broken, but he bore it like a man, except as the wagon would jolt he'd groan."

---Washington Mackey Ives, 4th Florida, Preston's Brigade

"We formed in line after wading the river, about six hundred yards from Round Forest, ... the Twentieth Tennessee Regiment on the right of the Brigade."

---W.J. McMurray, 20th Tennessee, Preston's Brigade

"As we formed in line of battle there was a Confederate, the first dead man I had yet seen, lying on his back with a cannon ball hole though his breast I could stick my head in."

---Ives, 4th Florida, Preston's Brigade

"Excited as I was, I looked around and thought: 'What an awfully sublime scene.' Wounded men were coming in a stream, dead were lying all around, and on every living face was ... the ... excitement which has no equal here on earth. All around us the smoke of battle had settled down, rent aside every moment by the thunder of artillery. ...

"The finest sight of all was our division ranged in order of battle, awaiting the comand 'forward.' We were formed across a high hill on perfectly open ground, so that every regiment could be seen. Our regiment formed the extreme right, resting on the river."

---Cooper, 20th Tennessee, Preston's Brigade

"About 2:30 our brigade was ordered ... to charge a battery supported by a mass of Federal infantry just across the railroad cut from where the Federal cemetery is now located."

---McMurray, 20th Tennessee, Preston's Brigade

"About the time we started forward the firing had almost ceased, and a most unearthly silence prevailed. We moved forward slowly at first, Preston's Brigade leading. When we had advanced two hundred yards, the (Union) sharpshooters commenced popping away, killing and wounding numbers of our men. Our walk then quickened to a run, and the whole line dashed forward with a shout."

---Cooper, 20th Tennessee, Preston's Brigade

"The enemy held their artillery fire until we started forward. ... We moved as if driven by a whirlwind, sweeping down by the Cowan house, and passed across the turnpike, leaving the railroad cut to our left.

"Just here the Twentieth ... became separated from the other four regiments of the brigade, ... which went to the left of the railroad cut and the Twentieth Tennessee went to the right in a straight line towards the Round Forest, from whence a heavy fire was emanating. ... After we passed the intersection of the railroad and the pike, we entered a cotton field about four hundred yards wide that lay in front of Round Forest. ... About half way it got so hot for us we were ordered to lie down, with nothing to protect us but cotton stalks.

"The Yankee Infantry had now turned loose on us, we couldn't go forward without reinforcements and they could not be gotten up to where we were, and we didn't want to go back, so we stayed there until it was useless to stay any longer. Colonel Smith having ordered us to fall back, and every man for himself, if ever you saw a lot of men get out of a place in quick time the Twentieth Tennessee Regiment did it, I being one of the foremost. ...

"(John Crocker) a neighbor boy who went to school with me and my mess mates in the army, was lying by my side, and when the order to retreat was given, he and I sprang up together and just as we had started to the rear, a minnie ball struck him in the upper part of his thigh and it seemed to me that he jumped four feet into the air and fell; his thigh bone was terribly shattered, and he fell into the hands of the enemy, and I never saw him any more until after the war. ... A number of our killed and wounded were left in the cotton field, we were so close under the enemy's guns that we could not bring them off.

"The Twentieth Tennessee fell back some three hundred yards, near the crossing of the Pike and railroad, everything was in confusion, our colonel wounded and our color bearer killed. ... Major (Fred) Claybrooke, who was on a very large horse, took one of our color guards by the name of Isaac Hyde up behind him with the colors, while under fire from the enemy's sharpshooters and artillery; he rode up and down our line, rallying our men until he restored order, and then faced them by the right flank, and double quicked them down under a bluff of rocks at the river edge. ... The regiment was here halted and faced the bluff and cotton field. ...

"The enemy had moved four or five hundred troops down across the cotton field in rear of the fence on the bluff. Major Claybrooke, when his regiment was sufficiently protected by the bluff, halted his men, faced them to the front, ordered them to fix bayonets, scale this bluff and drive the enemy back out of the cotton field."

---**McMurray, 20th Tennessee, Preston's Brigade**

"(Lt. Crosthwait) had a strange premonition that he would fall. ... When we were called upon to make that desperate charge from the Cowan House, he said to me: 'Ralph, I would willingly give a limb to be safely through this fight. I shall not come out of it. ... I feel the nearness of death. ...'

"We were very close friends, and I said to him: 'Frank, I would not go into this charge feeling as you do. You will not be criticised, for we all know your courage; and you are too useful a soldier to be spared.'

"But he replied, 'I would rather die a soldier than to live a coward.' "

---**Ralph J. Neal, 20th Tennessee, Preston's Brigade**

"The bluff ranged from six to ten feet high, and the highest part of the bluff was in front of the left wing of the regiment. When the order to charge was given those of us on the left wing had some trouble in scaling the bluff; ... We had to go up between two rocks. The first man was killed, the second wounded, and I was the third man but was not touched. ... As I cleared the crevice between the rocks, the enemy had fallen back, and a Federal soldier had gotten on the side of the fence next to our line and some one had killed him. I at once seized the dead Yankee's gun and fired at a retreating Federal not forty steps away, with a rest of the gun on the top rail of the fence. I don't think he even looked back.

"In scaling this bluff, we lost ... Lieutenant Frank Crosthwait of Company E. ...

"Before all of the left wing had gained the top of the bluff, the right ... had entered the cotton field and swung around to the left."

---**McMurray, 20th Tennessee, Preston's Brigade**

"Those in our front did not wait very long, but 'tuck the back track,' leaving us about thirty prisoners and numbers of wounded."

---**Cooper, 20th Tennessee, Preston's Brigade**

"The remainder fell back across the cotton field under the protection of their guns."

---**McMurray, 20th Tennessee, Preston's Brigade**

"A large proportion of our men had been wounded by this time, for they were falling at every step. We did not have more than one hundred and fifty left, and we had done all men could do and had to fall back, taking our prisoners."

---Cooper, 20th Tennessee, Preston's Brigade

(The rest of Preston's Brigade, which had gotten separated from the 20th Tennessee, also loses many killed and wounded in attacking the Round Forest:)

"The 4th had to pass through a picket fence, and in doing so we got our ranks broken and in forming, the 60th (North Carolina) ... crowded us so that we were all crowded out of place. And then 9 (companies) of the 60th turned and ran like sheep, leaving us under the hottest kind of fire from sharpshooters in front and 20 or 30 pieces of cannon about 1/2 mile distant on our right.

"We were halted under this fire and ordered to fire in the cedar thicket in front, and while we were driving the Yankee sharpshooters out of the wood the (Yankee) batteries got our range and then the men began to drop. ... John Hacker falls about a file to my left, and John McKinney ... had his throat cut at my right side. He fell on my feet and blood splattered in a stream as large as my two forefingers. Poor fellow, he could not speak, though he grabbed at the wound and tried to raise up.

"Phil Coates got shot through the right thigh. Elijah Linch got his head skinned by a ball, Little Billy Hinson got shot under the shoulders, sideways.

"We were then ordered into the thicket. ... The trees and limbs were falling thick, but on we went. The dead Yankees lay thick in the woods. We kept in the cedars and went on until we got to the edge or about 250 (yards) ... from where we entered, and then we could see the (Yankee) line of Battle 1,000 (yards north) ... of us. The Confederate batteries now began to fire on the yankees' batteries, which drew their fire from us, and thus things continued til dark."

---Ives, 4th Florida, Preston's Brigade

Sleeping with the Dead

(Behind the Union lines, wounded soldiers stream into field hospitals. Amandus Silsby, who had gotten separated from his unit and been ordered to help at one of the hospitals, finds plenty to do:)

"My first employment was helping dig graves and bury the dead. I helped bury eight. Afterward I was put into the rooms to take care of the wounded. Most all that had a limb amputated died."

---Silsby, 24th Wisconsin, Sill's Brigade

"Soon after I arrived at the hospitial a surgeon proposed to dress my wound; but I told him to attend to others around me, who needed attention first. ...

"It was impossible to supply all the wounded with tents. Rails were hauled and fires built, and they were laid on the ground before the fires. Men were wounded in ever conceivable way - some with their arms and legs shot off, some in the head, and some in the body. It was heart-rending to hear their cries and groans. ... I saw the surgeons amputate limbs, then throw the quivering flesh into a pile. Every once in a while a man would stretch himself out and die."

---Owens, 74th Ohio, Miller's Brigade

"There was scarcely more than an hour of sunshine left on that Wednesday, ... when the driver (helped me from) the ambulance ... at the field hospital of the Ninetieth Ohio. The large, square-made hospital tent was already becoming crowded. ...

"At the further end one of the surgeons was ... bandaging a ghastly wound in the arm of a poor wretch, the sleeve of whose blouse, cut away at the shoulder and all matted and stiff with gore, was lying on the ground beside him. ... Close by, and down upon one knee, was the chaplain, with a memorandum book and pencil, taking the sufferers' names with the commands to which they belonged, and the home address of the friends of each. ...

"The surgeon was soon ready for me, and proceeded to examine the wound. ... 'A very narrow escape, young man,' he said at length. ... 'A wound ... right through the base of the neck and behind the right clavicle, which it has evidently struck and fractured ..., and then glancing upward seems to have shattered the acromius. How the trachea escaped without most serious injury I can not see.' ...

"The wound was soon dressed, ... then a few fresh bundles of corn-blades were brought in, ... and on the bed that they made ... in one corner I sat down with a weary contentedness. ... About dusk our suppers were brought in - a cup of coffee and a biscuit."

---Ebenezer Hannaford, 6th Ohio, Grose's Brigade

"Sergeant (A.B.) Cosler ... procured an old blanket for me, and I lay by the fire all night. ... Although my leg pained me considerably, so that I slept very little during the night, still I did not complain, as there were others who were hurt a great deal worse than I was. ...

"One poor fellow, who was near me, was wounded in the head. He grew delirious during the night, and would frequently call for his mother. He would say, 'Mother, O mother, come and help me!' The poor fellow died before morning, with no mother near to soothe him in his dying moments or wipe the cold sweat from his brow. ...

"Oh, how often on that long and dreary night of the 31st of December, 1862, as I lay wounded on the ground, at the field hospital, with no covering but part of an old blanket ... did I think of my loving wife and dear mother at home."

---Owens, 74th Ohio, Miller's Brigade

"I could not sleep. ... So the night wore on - in thinking, waiting, wondering, in weariness and pain. The old year was passing away. We were dying together. It seemed hard so to die - by suffocation, I thought, from internal hemorrhage that was slowly filling my lungs with blood. Respiration was almost impossible, except in a sitting position, and propped nearly upright though I was, my breath came only with thick, irregular gasps. ...

"Toward morning there was ... relief of that horrible feeling of suffocation, and I dropped into a brief and broken slumber."

---Hannaford, 6th Ohio, Grose's Brigade

(On the battlefield, the grim night envelopes Rosecrans' weary troops:)

"That night wee was not allowed a fire and had nothing to eat and i spent New Years eve in a hole in the rocks where three of us had the smalest kind of fire."

---Weir, 25th Illinois, Woodruff's Brigade

"Soon after dark a small fire was built, and several of the men of the 21st had gathered about it, trying to get a little warmth. General Rosecrans came up and said, 'You are my men and I don't like to have any of you hurt. Where the enemy see a fire like this, they know twenty-five or thirty men are gathered about it, and are sure to shoot at it. I advise you to put it out.' Scarcely was he done speaking, when sure enough a line shot came just high enough to miss the heads of the party, and a shell exploded just beyond.

"About eleven o'clock we were permitted to go back out of range of the enemy's guns, build fires, and get supper, of which we were sorely in need; a hasty and scanty breakfast being the only sustenance we had had that day."

---Capt. Canfield, 21st Ohio, Miller's Brigade

"The night of the 31st a number of general officers were assembled by Rosecran's order, including McCook, Thomas, Stanley and myself.

"There was some talk of falling back. I do not remember who started the subject, but ... I (said) ... my men would be very much discouraged to have to abandon the field after their good fight of the day, during which they had uniformly held their position. ...

"Rosecran's called for McCook to accompany him on a ride, directing us to remain until their return.

"McCook (later) ... told me that the purpose of this ride was to find a position beyond Overall's Creek to which the army might retire. Upon approaching the creek, Rosecrans, perceiving mounted men moving up and down with torches, said to McCook: 'They have got entirely in our rear and are forming a line of battle by torchlight.'

"(Rosecrans and McCook) ... returned then to where we were, and Rosecrans told us to go to our commands and prepare to fight or die. The explanation of the torches is (our) ... men were making fires, and the torches were firing-brands being carried from one point to another by cavalrymen."

---Maj. Gen. Thomas L. Crittenden

(Behind the Confederate lines, wounded Rebels crowd into their field hospitals for treatment. On his way, Sgt. Garner pauses where his commander fell:)

"(I) passed by and examined Capt. Thomas, who was lying cold and stiff in a puddle of his own frozen blood; the ball entering one side of the neck, coming out the other, severing the arteries.

"When I reached the point from which I had started that morning I found about 50 men slightly wounded around a camp fire. All night long the ambulance and litter bearers were bearing the wounded by to the field hospital near us in the old McCullough farm house. I got one of the drivers ... to bring Capt. Thomas' corpse back to our campfire."

---Sgt. Garner, 25th Arkansas, McNair's Brigade

"Captain Kendrick and I were able to get to a Federal hospital that had been brought within our lines ... which was said to be the home of Mr. or General Smith, a wealthy planter near the Nolensville Pike. (It) was a large white house with numbers of smaller cabins on the outer edge of a beautiful yard, in one of which we found lodging for the night. ... A Federal surgeon kindly dressed our wounds and spoke words of comfort to us."

---Hutcherson, 3rd Georgia Battalion, Rains' Brigade

"We did not reach the line of battle that evening, and at sunset went to the hospital, in a church near the town. ... One little fellow in particular attracted my attention. 'O, sir, if you have a sharp knife, please cut this ball out of my hand! It is nearly killing me. The surgeon says there is no ball in my hand!' he cried in agony.

"Dr. B.F. Duggan, of Unionville, happened to come in about that time, and said to the sufferer: 'Let me see your hand.' ... The doctor soon found the ball and cut it out.

"Wandering over the battlefield that night, we reached the field hospital of the Twenty-Third Tennessee Regiment. Here I learned that my brother Richard had been wounded that evening, but I could not learn how severely."

---Moon, civilian

"I was severely wounded just before sunrise. ... I was taken to the hospital in Murfreesboro. So many wounded were there that I received no attention. One of the surgeons said: 'Don't fool with him now. In the morning we will take that arm off.'

" 'In the morning' I was not there, for soon after dark I crept out, took up an empty bucket, put my blanket over my wounded arm, and passed the guards as if I were going to the pump out on the street. With much difficulty I reached the depot and left on the first train going southward."

---James W. Ellis, 4th Arkansas, McNair's Brigade

(On the battleline, Preston's Brigade regroups after its failure to drive the bluecoats from the Round Forest:)

"It was now nearly dark, ... Claybrooke marched his Regiment and prisoners a few yards to the rear, where he received orders to rejoin his brigade nearly half a mile west in the cedar glade."

---McMurray, 20th Tennessee, Preston's Brigade

"We ... moved to the right, passing over many dead bodies, and in the darkness stepping on them before we knew it."

---Cooper, 20th Tennessee, Preston's Brigade

"When the roll was called that night, someone answered for ... (Lt. Crosthwait) 'Dead.' He was found lying with his face upturned and his feet toward the foe. His handkerchief was in his left hand. He had torn it in strips, knotted the pieces, and with it tried to stop the flow of blood from a severed artery; but, faint with loss of blood, he fell back, passing his bloody hand across his brow, and the end came.

"He fell before Murfreesboro, which had been his early home and the home of his ancestors, extending back to Col. Hardy Murfree, of Revolutionary (War) memory."

---Neal, 20th Tennessee, Preston's Brigade

"We were ordered back about 50 yards and broke ranks to sleep on arms, but it was very little sleeping that any of us did for I like to have died of the cold. My teeth chattered all night. We did not have our blankets, and the ground was frozen hard."

---Ives, 4th Florida, Preston's Brigade

"We lay down, but for a time sleep was impossible to men who had passed through such dreadful scenes that day and expected a renewal of them on the morrow. ... Many souls had passed into eternity that day."

---Cooper, 20th Tennessee, Preston's Brigade

"After dark the bodies of Brooks and Elliott were brought to the caissons. Both of them were killed by cannon shots. ... This was a gloomy night, ... with our dead comrades lying (in) our midst. ... The bivouac fires of the two armies (were) in view of each other."

---1st Sgt. Brown, Stanford's Mississippi Battery, Stewart's Brigade

"I rode over the field after night hunting some harness. The groans of the poor wounded was heartwrending. I could not repress a few falling tears. I got off my horse and built fires for several - foe and friend. Many, many ... chilled to death ... that night might have been saved could they but have had attendance."

---Cpl. Magee, Stanford's Mississippi Battery, Stewart's Brigade

"We built fires that night and slept on the frozen ground. About midnight another soldier and I got up to warm. The moon was shining brightly. He proposed that we go to that cedar brake and see why the Yankees stopped firing so quickly. We went, and such a sight I had never seen. The havoc our guns had made was appalling."

---M'Dearman, 12th Tennessee, Vaughan's Brigade

"We were ordered ... to furnish a detail of forty men ... to go on picket. I was detailed as the officer of the pickets. ... A staff officer ... led us through the thick cedars where Cheatham and his Tennesseeans had fought over during the day, and the ground was strewn with the dead and wounded. ... No one was in front of us but the Yankees and they were about one hundred yards away.

"My line being established, it was my duty ... to visit the different picket posts at intervals during the night. The night was cold and clear, the ground frozen to the depth of about one inch.

"While I was making my rounds, about one o'clock a.m., I heard quite a halloahing and moaning some fifty yards in the rear. ... I crept back up a little rocky ravine ... and discovered, as I had expected, a wounded soldier. I asked, 'To what command do you belong?'

"He said Eighteenth Regulars and that he was badly wounded and had been left here and was nearly frozen to death. He asked me to make him a fire at his feet. I told him I was a Confederate and on picket just in front of him, and by making a fire would draw the picket fire from the Yankee's post.

"He begged me so pitifully, and as he was down in a ravine, I took the chances, and searched around among the rocks and got some cedar limbs and made him a fire and gave him some water, placed his head on his knapsack and made him as comfortable as possible. ... The poor fellow had bled and laid on the ground until life was nearly gone. ...

"I went back in about two hours, but he had crossed over (died) ... and I could do no more for him."

---McMurray, 20th Tennessee, Preston's Brigade

There was a large lime sink (hole) four or five feet deep where my company was stationed. This afforded protection from the wind, which was very cold, and we built little fires in there, as they could not be seen by the enemy.

"Among the wounded we put in our resort was a Yank quite young and intelligent, shot centrally through the breast with a Minie ball. We divided water and rations with him, and next morning our young Yank, with assistance to rise, could sit up awhile."

---Lt. Tunnell, 14th Texas, Ector's Brigade

New Year's Day

"Thursday morning the sun arose without clouds, but along the eastern horizon was a broad zone of mist and fog through which the great luminary looked red and bloody."

---Owens, 74th Ohio, Miller's Brigade

(About 40 miles to the southeast, just outside McMinnville, in the home of Mrs. Virginia French:)

"It is a brilliant, sunshining morning, cold, clear, and bracing - a heavy white frost lay on the ground when I awoke. The sun rose in a crimson and amber sky - and when I look - I see the ther(mometer) at 32 ... in the hall. ...

"We expected the battle would be renewed this morning and we listened earnestly for the cannonading, but we have heard none as yet. ... We trust the Yankees have given way, and fallen back to Nashville."

---L. Virginia French

(On the battlefield, Moon and his young sight-seeing companions also expect fighting to resume:)

"One of our company dismounted, and, divesting a dead Federal soldier of knapsack, pistols, gun, and all accouterments, armed himself as a soldier. When questioned, he said: 'I am going to fight today if the battle opens up.' "

---Moon, civilian

"The Forty-second, with the brigade, took its regular place in the center proper, and on the front line. ... From morning to noon, and from noon till night, the rebels were feeling our line. On the right a feint would be made, then on the left, then on the center; and thus on through the whole day, but no general attack was made.

"The horseshoe shape of our line gave great advantage to our army. Reinforcements could be thrown in a very brief time from right to left - from the hollow of this formation to the center or anywhere, the distance being then from our right to our left not to exceed three-fourths of a mile at any time."

---Capt. Horrall, 42nd Indiana, J. Beatty's Brigade

"Our baggage-wagons ... (had been) attacked and driven back, so that we had no tents or cooking-utensils, and with but little or nothing to eat - only hard crackers and middling-meat, called, in army parlance, 'Hard-tack and sow-belly.' "

---Col. Moody, commander 74th Ohio, Miller's Brigade

"Rations were distributed as far as possible, but in many cases the commissary trains had been either delayed or destroyed by the enemy's cavalry. The cracker supply having been cut off, it was necessary to distribute flour instead of crackers.

"Each man in the Regiment drew a certain quantity of flour, and the facilities for turning this into bread or anything edible were exceedingly primitive. ... You might have seen soldiers making dough of flour, water and salt, and baking it on a stone laid on hot coals."

---Gibson, 78th Pennsylvania, Miller's Brigade

"As our brigade lay in reserve ..., late in the day an officer's horse was killed by a cannon ball ..., and before the blood had ceased to circulate in the animal, so hungry were the boys that they cut steaks from the dead animal and broiled them for supper."

---Capt. Horral, 42nd Indiana, J. Beatty's Brigade

(Alexander Pepper, wounded while defending the angle in the Union line against Rebel assaults, and Ira Owens, hit in the leg when the Union center was pushed back, find little consolation in their field hospitals:)

"My arm was quite sore and swollen. I saw that I would have to pay a little attention to it so I went to taking care of it myself. I was my own Doctor. My remedy was cold water; I sat and kept a pail of cold water and a rag and kept a stream running on it nearly all day and I reduced the swelling."

---Pepper, 59th Illinois, Post's Brigade

"Having no shelter-tent, it was very disagreeable. ... Rows of men were laid out side by side, ready for the soldier's burial. ... They were wrapped in the soldier's blanket, a trench dug, their bodies placed side by side, like they fought, a few shovelfuls of earth thrown upon them and they were left alone."

---Owens, 74th Ohio, Miller's Brigade

(On the other side, Rebel troopers gather their dead and wounded:)

"Contrary to our expectation, there was no fighting this day, but some very lively skirmishing. ... (The) night had been very cold, and numbers of the wounded had perished. ...

"I had been detailed 'on the infirmary corps,' and was busily occupied all the morning bringing in the wounded, both Confederate and Federal. I walked over the battle field and saw some terrible sights. In one place two brothers were lying dead, both killed by the same shell."

---Cooper, 20th Tennessee, Preston's Brigade

"A temporary armistice was gotten up ... to bury the dead, and to further care for the more seriously wounded. A few Federal surgeons had crossed the line under a flag of truce ... to attend their wounded, who had been brought ... to our field hospital.

"The weather was bitter cold that morning. The dead on the field ... were actually frozen."

---**Robuck, 29th Mississippi, P. Anderson's Brigade**

"Not being able to procure a coffin or even a plank for a box of any kind, I and Yon Stanly and some one else of our Co. & John Lockey of Capt. Hammond's Co. ... procured an ambulance (and) took ... (Capt. Thomas) and Capt. Hammond a short distance to the McCullough family graveyard & the boys, though all slightly wounded, dug a deep wide grave in the S.E. corner of the graveyard. ...

"I, not being able to walk, sat by a fire & carved with my knife each one's name on hard seasoned pieces of oak plank & placed them at their respective heads."

---**Garner, 25th Arkansas, McNair's Brigade**

"At daylight ... Gen. Preston marched us deeper into the cedars so we could build small fires and be warm. ... The Yankees threw a great many shells at us, one cut Lt. Harris' ... haversack and went through his coat; it wounded two men in Miot's Co. ... We lay in this thicket all day among the dead and dying Yankees. I slept at night a little, for Col. Bowen got our blankets for us."

---**Ives, 4th Florida, Preston's Brigade**

"There was a great deal of pilfering performed on the dead bodies of the Yankees by our men. Some of them were left as naked as they were born, everything in the world they had being taken from them.

"I ordered my men to take their fine guns and canteens if they wished, but nothing else. ... The only thing I took was a fine canteen which I cut off a dead Yankee who was lying on his face in our path as we marched along."

---**James B. Mitchell, 34th Alabama, Manigault's Brigade**

(Meanwhile, in the Rebel field hospitals:)

"About 10 o'clock that morning I went to our field hospital to talk with members of my company who were there wounded. ... I was attracted by an argument between an Irish Yankee soldier and a Federal Surgeon. The Irishman was ... begging the surgeon not to amputate his ... foot, ... the ankle bone ... had been fractured. ...

"Soon the surgeon had my entire attention. There was something strangely familiar about his features. ...

"The Irishman was on an improvised operating table ... of rough poplar planks resting on heavy wood forks. So I concluded to walk up near the table. ... Another surgeon approached the table, and after examining the wound said: 'I fail to find the necessity for an amputation in this case, Brooks.'

"Ah! ... He was Doctor Brooks, the brute that had so cruelly overpowered and beaten me so unmercifully in Philadelphia. He was now surgeon for an Ohio regiment.

"He appeared now very different from what he was two years before. He was not so robust, and I had noticed him take frequent drinks from a flask drawn from his coat pocket. While he had lost, I had gained, and weighed now one hundred and seventy-five pounds, in perfect health, and felt stout as a mule.

"I stepped in front of him and asked: 'Are you Doctor Brooks?' Waving his hand and bowing, he replied: 'I have the honor, sir.' 'You also have the honor of having whipped me once in the city of Philadelphia,' (I said,) 'and now since we have met again I propose to renew the contest.'

"He eyed me a moment, in evident surprise, then asked bluntly, 'Are you Robuck?' Bowing politely and waving my hand in mimicry of his own style, I replied, 'I have the honor, sir.'

"He hastily placed his instruments on the table, drew forth his flask, swallowed a draught of brandy, drew off and threw aside his coat and rushed at me like a maniac. Being ... about three-fourths drunk, he ... was not strictly on his guard. ... I knocked him down, and ... held him down ... and pounded him until he acknowledged that he was whipped.

"In the meantime his Irish patient had raised up on the table and kept calling out to me, 'Give it to 'im, Johnnie Reb; kill 'im and save me leg; maul 'im good.' "

---Robuck, 29th Mississippi, P. Anderson's Brigade

"(At Col. Smith's house) ... with arm in sling I strolled over the yard, where lay in rows hundreds of Federal dead, with narrow aisles between along which one might walk and read the name, company, regiment, and State of each. Oftentimes the simple word 'unknown' was pinned upon the dead soldier's breast. On the outer edge of this yard a long ditch was being dug the size of a large grave, but of great length. ...

"From that veritable charnel house (Capt. Kendrick and I) ... made our way to Murfreesboro, where confusion reigned supreme. Thousands of prisoners and wounded ... occupied the town. ... We saw in the town the long black casket containing the body of our beloved General Rains."

---Hutcherson, 3rd Georgia Battalion, Rains' Brigade

"I spent most of the day searching for my fallen brother, but all in vain. He sleeps among the unknown dead. I went home."

---Moon, civilian

(Near McMinnville, Mrs. Virginia Smith is stunned to learn a friend in Bragg's army was killed in Wednesday's fighting. Capt. Drury C. 'Cap' Spurlock of the 16th Tennessee had been a merchant in McMinnville before the war. The night of Dec. 30 his mother and father had traveled from McMinnville to Murfreesboro to visit him. The 30-year-old captain had gotten a few hours of leave on the eve of the battle and spent them with his parents, who were staying in the Miles Hotel:)

"After supper we were all sitting in the back room when Cooper came to the door and said 'Mas' John, Mr. Spurlock has just come from Murfreesboro en' he wants you to come. ... Mr. Cap Spurlock is killed and they are bringing his body up now.' ...

"I felt as if stunned by a thunder-bolt. 'Cap' Spurlock killed! I could not believe it. ... We all three, Mollie, Darlin' (Virginia's husband), and myself went up immediately. ...

"('Cap') was in the hottest part of the fight - his company was stationed on both sides of the R.R. just where it crossed the pike, near Cowan's (house). He was acting as Maj. - (Pat Coffe being here at home on sick furlough,) and had sprange on in advance of his men, cheering him on, when he was struck down. ...

"The ball entered just below the left nostril, and passed through his head stopping just under the skin. ...

"It was 11 o'clock at night (Wednesday, Dec. 31) before his body was recovered. His father was there - he had gone down with a wagon to carry the boys Christmas things - and he brought back the body of his son!

"We went into the parlor at John's to see poor Cap, as soon as he was laid out. His uniform was very bloody and had to be cut off him - they had dressed him in a fine suit of black cloth such as he used to wear before the war began. ... You could not notice the small place where the ball entered, it was concealed by his mustache. ...

"About 10 o'clock they took him down to town to his mother. Darlin' went with the corpse and remained all night."

---L. Virginia French

Breckinridge's Charge

(Friday morning, Jan. 2, 1863, the two armies still face each other. This is the day that will decide the Battle of Stones River:)

"(There was a) hill or prominence ... on the left flank of the Federal army, which, could it be taken and held by the Confederate forces, would necessitate the evacuation of the Federal position or otherwise force a general engagement.

"The reconnoisance showed there were no troops of any kind in sight, though the hill was of sufficient prominence to hide from view a considerable force. The fact that a picket line was in front, and the apparent importance of the position from a strategic point of view, was prima facie evidence of such a force being ready to defend it. ...

"A message came from General Bragg for General Breckinridge to report at his temporary headquarters, a few hundred yards in the rear on the river bank. ... Bragg's orders to Breckinridge were that a vigorous attack on the position just reconnoitered should be carried, held and strongly fortified, having in view positions for four field batteries.

"Besides the three batteries from his own division, he had been assigned Captain Robinson's Battery of Napoleons from Polk's Corps.

"The hour of attack was to be about four o'clock, the signal being a discharge of four pieces of artillery in quick succession. The impression appeared to be that with an attack at that hour, if successful, the enemy would not attempt to retake it that night, giving ample time to fortify.

"The balance of the army at the signal were to make demonstrations with artillery and otherwise along the whole front. These instructions were given in my hearing at about noon on January 2.

"Breckinridge began at once to make the necessary preparations. ... On my expression to Breckinridge a wish to see the movement through, he promptly acquiesced, and gave me temporary assignment on his staff."

---Col. Pickett, Hardee's assistant inspector general

"We were all pretty certain that we would go to the rear to rest and warm a little after being relieved in the Cedars, but no such luck, tis true they carried us where it was warm enough but nary rest. They took us back across the river near to our first position and pitched us right into the Yanks before we knowed what we were about, and I tell you I never want to go into another such fight as long as I live."

---William D. Rogers, 1st Florida, Preston's Brigade

"Heaps of unburied dead lay in the cornfields. We kept on through the fields and woods until we came to the east of the Yankees, having

Confederate view of McFadden's Ford, the turning point. (Battlefield tour stop 9.)

been to the southwest of them. We formed line of battle in an old field."

---Ives, 4th Florida, Preston's Brigade

"At (Breckinridge's) ... orders, I formed the two right brigades, Pillow (in command of Palmer's Brigade) in front, supported by W.C. Preston's Brigade in the second line. On the left of Pillow was Hanson's Kentucky Brigade, supported by (Pegram's dismounted cavalry brigade)."

---Col. Pickett, Hardee's assistant inspector general

"The First Kentucky Brigade, commanded by Gen. Hanson, was marched to the front and drawn up into line opposite the opening of a bend in Stone's river, which nearly formed a horseshoe. The Federal forces occupied the North side ... and we the South, except at this narrow opening, where their lines crossed over, occupying this space of about a quarter of a mile. ... We had watched from day to day the construction of these works, little dreaming that we would be called on to storm them. Two other lines were formed in the rear."

---Jervis D. Grainger, 6th Kentucky, Hanson's Brigade

"The four batteries of artillery were in the rear at a proper interval, and were to go into action at the proper time. Everything was apparently well screened from the view of the enemy."

---Col. Pickett, Hardee's assistant inspector general

(Across the way, Yankee brigades in Gen. Van Cleve's division await the attack:)

"Near the hour of noon the enemy were seen moving into the woods and forming in massed column."

---Sgt. Samuel Welch, 51st Ohio, Price's Brigade

"Our brigade was located on the edge of a stretch of timber, and in our immediate front was an immense corn field of probably 75 acres. The corn had been husked on the stalks, and the stalks still stood dead and dry."

---Samuel Mullet, 51st Ohio, Price's Brigade

(Rosecrans begins moving other Union brigades into positions behind Van Cleve:)

"About noon ... a part of a ration of flour was issued to the men, with the admonition to prepare and eat it as soon as possible. Some made paste, sweetened and drank it, others made dough, and in every conceivable way without utensils tried to bake it. Some ate the dough partly baked, and when the order 'fall in' was given, some snatched theirs from the fire and others went away dinnerless, leaving theirs behind unbaked. The regiment, with the rest of Negley's division, went on the 'double quick' about a mile and a half, filled their canteens, and laid down on the right bank of Stone's River to await the assault of the enemy."

---Capt. Canfield, 21st Ohio, Miller's Brigade

"That Friday my dear mother made her way to Murfreesboro through the Confederate pickets to look after husband and sons. ... (In) ... a letter she wrote of this trip:

" 'On entering (Murfreesboro) ... what a sight met my eyes! Prisoners entering every street, ambulances bringing in the wounded, every place crowded with the dying, the Federal general, Sill, lying dead in the courthouse - killed Wednesday - Frank Crosthwait's (Twentieth Tennessee) lifeless corpse stretched on a counter. He had been visiting my house, and was killed on Wednesday. The churches were full of wounded, where the doctors were amputating legs and arms. I found my (husband and sons) ... safe, and, being informed that another battle was expected to begin, I set off on my way home, and passed through our cavalry all drawn up in line. I had only gone a mile when the first cannon boomed, but I was safe.' "

---Ridley, civilian

(At about the same time, 40 miles to the southeast, in McMinnville:)

"Friday afternoon we attended the funeral (of 'Cap' Spurlock). ... In his coffin ... a garland of geranium and evergreen was laid all around his head and shoulders. ... The frantic exclamations of his mother - the half frightened and wild sobbing of poor Florence (his sister) - and the still silent agony of the aged father were terrible. ... As Miss Sophia Searcy stood for hours beside his coffin, weeping, I wondered if she remembered the time when she had said, - 'Let the war come! I want it to come! I want these Tennessians roused - let it come - we are ready.' Were any of us ready to part with 'Cap'?

"The artillery firing at Murfreesboro was tremendous that evening, heavier and faster than we ever heard it - and it was heard as Mr. McMurray prayed. ... All the way to the grave-yard - and while we laid ("Cap") ... down to his last rest - and as we returned - it came rolling up from the northwest."

---L. Virginia French

"About 4 oclock got orders for all batteries to shell the woods in front vigoursly, and draw the enemy's attention while Breckinridge made an attack on our right. The enemy replied heavily. ... Louder and louder was the roar of the canon, while far to the right, that once more incessant and deafening clash of musketry was heard."

---Cpl. Magee, Stanford's Mississippi Battery,
Steawart's Brigade

"The roar of four pieces of artillery gave the signal."

---Cooper, 20th Tennessee, Preston's Brigade

"The colors went up, ... and we stepped forward. ... We were at the foot of a gradual incline, the enemy at the top of the ridge. We advanced steadily, ... as did the two columns behind us. Batteries right and left ... commenced playing upon us, but as yet we were not in range of those in front. ... Comrades were falling on either hand as we advanced at full run ... under orders not to fire until we reached the ... breastworks."

---Grainger, 6th Kentucky, Hanson's Brigade

"About four o'clock a furious charge was made on Van Cleve's division on the south side of the river, not far from where the river turns eastward at nearly a right angle. ... Enemy ... batteries opened a very heavy fire on us, to which our batteries replied. Shells, solid shot and grape shot were flying thick, but we were comparatively safe, being protected by the crest of the hill. ... General Negley rode along our lines, and being cheered by his troops, said in reply, 'Boys, you will now have an opportunity to pay them back for what they did on Wednesday.' "

---Gibson, 78th Pennsylvania, Miller's Brigade

"Gen. Palmer sent me on an errand ... through a line of our artillery posted on the west bluff of Stone River. On my return trip, when riding through the line and within ten or fifteen feet of one of the guns, I saw the axle cut from under it by a shot from the enemy. The beautiful brass gun tumbled to the ground. ... Shells were exploding and shrieking through the air. Solid shot was plowing the earth and throwing the ground in showers around us. ... Rifled and musket balls were doing their share of execution also.

"After passing the line of guns, I found myself among the artillerymen and horses, where an alarming confusion was found, caused by the fearful ... enemy's fire. ... When near one of the artillerymen, on his horse, I saw the upper part of his head disappear. A cannon shot did the work, and he fell from his horse a corpse."

---Henry Harrison Eby, 7th Illinois Cavalry

"(At) 4 p.m. ... I was ordered to bring the limbers of the caissens to the Battery to supply it with ammunition. The Battery was ... under a very heavy fire (from) ... several Yankee Batteries ... on account of having to fire the signal for the advance of Breckenridge's men and to attract the attention of the enemy. ...

"We went in at a trot and each team took position behind its respective gun, the riders dismounting and getting as close to the ground as convenient. In a few moments the ammuntion was transfered to the gun limbers, and I was ordered to retire. ... During the few moments we were under this fire, two of my squad and three or four of our horses were wounded. One of the men was lifted completely from his horse by the explosion of a shell, and landed several feet off on the ground, still he was not seriously hurt.

"The shells seemed to explode amongst us every second, and there was not an instant that a shot did not hiss by. Before I dismounted, my little bay horse had his hind leg nearly torn off by a piece of shell that seemed to burst in six feet of my face. At the order to retire I remounted him and his last act of service was to carry me out of danger. A hundred yards or so from the guns I dismounted and led on after the limbers. ...

"At our former position, I took my bridle and saddle off my wounded horse and put them on a spare horse. As the faithful animal stood there bleeding and shivering with pain, and I powerless to help him in return for the great service he had rendered me at Shiloh, I could not (keep from crying) ..., and when we drove off and left him, I could not have felt it more keenly had I been leaving a wounded human friend.

"I never saw him again. I suppose he died near the place I left him."

---Brown, Stanford's Mississippi Battery, Stewart's Brigade

"(Yankee) sharpshooters had been cracking away pretty briskly in our front, and we had gone only a short distance when their line was discovered, reaching away to the right of us, and outflanking us. This was more than we expected, but the line moved steadily on. ... As we entered an open stubble field, several hundred yards wide, the enemy being in the woods on the other side, the whole line, both artillery and small arms opened upon us with a deafening roar."

---Cooper, 20th Tennessee, Preston's Brigade

"Wright's Battery was rushed up in support. ... The front line of Yankees poured a volley into the Twentieth Regiment that made them stagger and waver like a drunken man. ... William Nevins, who was just on my left, lost his leg from this volley.

"The regiment pressed forward to the fence and had orders to lie down behind it. This put the two lines about forty yards apart, the Yankees were standing, and we were lying behind the fence. We had the advantage, and the slaughter was terrible.

"I carried an Enfield rifle in this charge, and at this fence I dropped down in a corner that no other Confederate happened to be in and saw three Federals standing by an oak tree. While I was laying as flat as I could in the fence corner, one of them shot at me and knocked off a piece of rail across my back. I returned the fire with a good rest on the rail for my gun. Another one shot at me and tore off a large portion of rail against my left breast, and by this time I had fired three shots, and the order was given to charge.

"The Regiment did not take time to climb the fence, but caught the fence about the third rail from the bottom, and the fence, line and all went over together. The first line of Yankees fell back to their second, we pressed them so closely, in twenty minutes the whole mass was going back to the river, and the whole Federal force that lapped us so far on our right, with no one in front of them except Wright's Battery that was shooting at them from a right oblique, fell back.

"As the Twentieth Regiment passed over the fence, we were soon upon the ground that was occupied by the front line of Federals, and it was the straightest and prettiest line of dead Yankees I ever saw. ... Every one of the color guards of the Twentieth Regiment had gone down except Frank Battle, a son of our first colonel. ... The color staff had been shot in two twice, and the colors were so heavy that the boy could scarcely carry them. He fell down on the ground, and we thought he, too, was killed, when Capt. W.T. Ridley of Company E., sprang forward to pick them up, when young Battle said, 'I just laid down to tie them to a portion of the staff,' and by this time the line overtook him, when he had wrapped the colors around him and was again in front.

"We were now crowding them back to the river on their masked batteries."

---McMurray, 20th Tennessee, Preston's Brigade

"As Breckinridge in beginning the advance emerged from the woods, the front line was at full charge. Hanson's Brigade, on the left, was more in view as it passed up over a rise in the field and presented a fine sight, as at 'right shoulder shift,' arms 'glistening in the sunlight,' giving rousing cheers as they 'double-quicked' up the slope.

"General Breckinridge ... exclaimed, pointing to the left: 'Look at old Hanson!' We ... proceeded along a line of fence ... about two-thirds the distance across the open when a halt was observed. On investigating the cause there, just over the fence was General Breckinridge kneeling by (Hanson's) ... side ... holding firmly to the artery of the leg just above the knee. The wounded man had ... received his death wound, as it afterwards came out that a large fragment of a shell had struck the leg just above the knee. ...

"Presently an officer rode up, followed by an ambulance, with tears streaming down his cheeks. It was Captain Helm, General Hanson's brother-in-law and his brigade commissary."

---Col. Pickett, Hardee's assistant inspector general

"(The Rebels') massed column emerged from the woods and moved forward rapidly, across the valley and up the hill on which we were situated. ... Our pickets were soon driven in, and as they took their places in the line they would say: 'Boys, they are coming, the woods are full of them.'

"We were ordered to lie down flat on the ground, so that the enemy's volley would pass over our heads. Lieutenant Colonel McClain passed quietly along the line, telling us to hold our fire until we were sure that we could make every shot tell. 'Don't rise,' said he, 'until you can see their hats as they come over the hill and then rise and fire.' On came the enemy in steady massed column. When their first line was almost to the top of the hill they raised the rebel yell, which they always made in an attack. All at once their hats were seen. They were then within twenty yards of us. Suddenly we arose and fired a volley simultaneously with a volley from their front line. Twenty-one of the Fifty-First fell dead and twenty-one fell mortally wounded in this one volley. ... Thirty dead Confederates were found by the line of the regiment where we were attacked, when we returned an hour later.

"When the sudden shock of this double volley was over, it seemed to me that both lines ... were annihilated, and before I had time to notice who had fallen their second line came over the ridge."

---Sgt. Welch, 51st Ohio, Price's Brigade

"Within ten minutes I had been shot, the ball passing between the two bones of my leg and coming out on the opposite side. ... We retreated some twenty feet, and then every thing grew dark to me and I dropped helplessly to the ground."

---Mullet, 51st Ohio, Price's Brigade

"Having a horror of being taken prisoner, and while the chances were against getting away safely, I suddenly decided to try."

---Sgt. Welch, 51st Ohio, Price's Brigade

"The enemy began to flee like blackbirds. ... We mounted their works from end to end and poured ... a deadly volley into the ... flying enemy. It was terrific! The ground for a hundred yards was

covered with their fallen. Another and another volley was fired as they ascended the slight rise from the works."

---**Grainger, 6th Kentucky, Hanson's Brigade**

"I was shot through the right thigh with a Minie ball soon after starting after the retreating enemy. I was the last of the color guards to fall. George Lowe, the color bearer, was ... falling ... when I caught hold of the flagstaff ..., and received my first wound, and we fell together. Capt. Nat Gooch then took the flag ... and was soon shot down. Logue Nelson, of Murfreesboro, then took the flag and carried it safely through the battle."

---**Cpl. McKay, 18th Tennessee, Palmer's Brigade**

"In a few minutes I regained consciousness but the Union line had gone. Just in front, on our first line, I saw Nathan Shannon ... sitting against a tree. He had evidently been seriously wounded. ... Dragging myself back to him just as the Confederate line swept out of the corn field, an old fellow fired point blank at us within a few feet. The wonder is that one or the other of us was not killed.

"I shouted to him, asking him if he wanted to shoot a dead man and just then the boys in gray crowded about us, giving us water out of their canteens and asking what command we belonged to. We told them, whereupon one of the Confederates said 'Bully for the Buckeyes,' and then all of them charged through the woods."

---**Mullet, 51st Ohio, Price's Brigade**

"Running as fast as possible and arriving at our second line of battle ... I fell in with our second line and fired several rounds, but the enemy came down through the woods line after line."

---**Sgt. Welch, 51st Ohio, Price's Brigade**

"Van Cleves' division, which had been stationed over the river, terrified at the onslaught of the rebels, delivered their fire, and retreated in haste, and great disorder. Men and horses a commingled mob; horses with riders and horses without - men with guns and men without, all making haste to escape, the enemy pursuing vigorously and pouring a destructive fire into the retreating mass."

---**Capt. Canfield, 21st Ohio, Miller's Brigade**

(Far on the Union right, brigades dug in along the Nashville Pike sense a crisis is brewing on the left end of Rosecrans' line:)

"As the volume of musketry increases, and the sound grows nearer, we understand that our troops are being driven back, and brigade after brigade double-quicks from the right and center, across the open field, to render aid.

"Battery after battery goes in the same direction on the run, the drivers lashing the horses to their utmost speed. The thunder of the guns becomes more violent; the volleys of musketry grow into one prolonged and unceasing roll."

---Col. J. Beatty, brigade commander

"Our General caled us out to help ... (a) division which was hard presed. They were on the left and great many of ... (the) men was runing away. Wee stoped some of them. We formed and started and had to wade the river thre times. It (was) over knee deep. Wee had to run about two miles. It was mudy and quite darke but wee got their while the fight was ragin."

---Weir, 25th Illinois, Woodruff's Brigade

(As Rosecrans rushes reinforcements to his left, Breckinridge's brigades continue to drive the Yankees before them to the river:)

"The river where we crossed was sixty feet wide and two feet deep. On the opposite side was a rocky bluff twenty feet high. As we were climbing up this bluff we could hear the enemy's bullets striking the rocks. My idea was that the army of the Cumberland was rapidly passing out of existence and that the Union cause was hopelessly lost. When we reached the top of the bluff we found that General Negley's divison was quietly lying in massed column in a cornfield, ready to move into action."

---Sgt. Welch, 51st Ohio, Price's Brigade

"We reformed and went forward down the bend of the river through a grove of heavy timber. More than half way to the river, I, with ten or twelve comrades, became detached. Pushing on and crossing to the enemy's side, we stopped to await our (division's) ... advance.

"I noticed a cabin to my left, on the high bank of the river about sixty yards away, the door and an open window fairly bristling with guns pouring ... fire into our men on the opposite side. Being sheltered by the body of a large sycamore, I ... fired eight or ten rounds (when) a roar of artillery commenced and continued for more than ten minutes, which shook the earth under my feet.

"I looked in the direction from which I had come. Such a dense cloud of smoke enveloped the troops and forest that scarcely a man was discernible."

---Grainger, 6th Kentucky, Hanson's Brigade

"The sound judgment ... of Maj. John Mendenhall, ... my chief-of-artillery, enabled me to open 58 guns almost simultaneously on Breckenridge's men, and to turn a dashing charge into a sudden retreat and route, in which the enemy lost 1700 or 1800 men in a few moments. ... Mendenhall's guns were about 100 yards back from the river. Van Cleve's division of my command was retiring down the opposite slope, before overwhelming numbers of the enemy, when the guns ... opened upon the swarming enemy. The very forest seemed to fall ... and not a Confederate reached the river."

---Maj. Gen. Thomas L. Crittenden

"As the mass of men swarmed down the slope they were mowed down by the score. Confederates were pinioned to the earth by falling branches. For a few minutes the brave fellows held their ground, hoping to advance, but the west bank bristled with bayonets."

---Lt. Col. G.C. Kniffin, Gen. Crittenden's staff

"Our batteries had exhausted their ammunition and, limbering, galloped to the rear. Then our Regiment, being the first in General Miller's brigade, was ordered forward. Shot and shell and minie balls were flying very thick when we reached the crest of the hill, but we opened fire at once and were followed by other regiments of our brigade. Only a few moments had elapsed when the shout went up, 'They are retreating! They are retreating!' ... Men and officers moved forward in double quick, crossed the river and drove the enemy before them."

---Gibson, 78th Pennsylvania, Miller's Brigade

"I fell in with Negley's division and re-crossed the river and advanced to the top of the hill where we were attacked."

---Sgt. Welch, 51st Ohio, Price's Brigade

"I proceeded with (firing) ... upon the men in the cabin. (After) twenty-five or thirty rounds from my trusty Enfield ... a brass band on my right attracted my attention. ... I saw a line, five or six columns deep, advancing to cross the shoal. In the direction I had left our men, not one was to be seen. Our (division) ... had retreated. ...

"Passing around my tree and drawing my gun down in line with the staff of the color bearer, I fired. The flag dropped to one side. I shot down the river bank ... (to) a bluff. ... I leaped as far as possible and dropped into the water to my armpits. ... The Yankees on whom I had fired were crossing just above me and the command 'Halt!' 'Halt!' was repeated ... and bang, bang came from ... (their) guns. ...

"Reaching the other shore I took up a double-quick. ... I lay down behind a tree and, raising my feet, rested them against its trunk to empty the water from my boots. Then to my feet again. ... Just as I was ... capturing a large dappled-gray riderless horse ... dashing by to my left, a cannon shot severed its head. ... On I went."

---Grainger, 6th Kentucky, Hanson's Brigade

"(The Rebels) came back on the run, taking their wounded with them. Comrade Shannon and I were now in range of our own guns and we crept round on the opposite side of two trees for shelter."

---Mullet, 51st Ohio, Price's Brigade

"Four men were carrying a wounded soldier on a litter. Another cannon ball whistled past me, striking the litter diagonally, killing one at either corner and the man whom they were carrying. The two remaining men joined me and together we reached our command ... at the edge of the timber where our lines were first formed."

---Grainger, 6th Kentucky, Hanson's Brigade

"I remained helpless and partially unconscious until our command retreated. I saw the Yankees coming and attempted to get up, but could not. Our men moved up a battery of three guns and planted them just over where I lay. The fire from the guns was nearly hot enough to burn my face; the Yankees' bullets rattled on the gun carriages like hail, and our men were forced to leave the guns, as they did not have horses enough to take them away."

---Cpl. McKay, 18th Tennessee, Palmer's Brigade

"The Twentieth Tennessee Regiment was among the last to leave the bank of the river, and Wright's gallant battery was still with us, so when we did start back the enemy was so close upon us, that we could not get all the battery off, so we lost the only guns that were lost in the engagement. ...

"(The battery's) gallant Captain E. Eldridge Wright was killed, his First Lieutenant, J.W. Mebane was wounded, but succeeded in getting off a portion of his battery. The brave battery had lost so heavily that in the retreat it did not have enough men to get all its guns away.

"One gun had only one boy left and he was not able to limber up his piece. He had fought it ... until the enemy was so close to him to remain longer would be death or capture, and he gave it up. This young lad was Luke E. Wright, a brother of the Battery's heroic Captain. He served gallantly through the war and ... (afterwards became) Governor of the Phillippine Islands."

---McMurray, 20th Tennessee, Preston's Brigade

"After the battery was deserted, I ... received my second wound from a bombshell fired by the Confederates, breaking my left arm and terribly bruising my body, from the concussion, I was told by the surgeon. I received several other slight wounds on my legs."

---Cpl. McKay, 18th Tennessee, Palmer's Brigade

"When we were about 150 yards from the battery, General Miller ordered the 78th Regiment to charge, ... the 19th Illinois, 69th Ohio and other regiments joining with us.

"We captured a battery of four guns, two of them being secured by our regiment. We captured also the colors of the 26th Tennessee Infantry. The captured flag was seized, I believe, at the same time by Private Davis of Company I and Private Hughes of Company B.

"The picture ... entitled 'The Charge of the 78th Regiment' ... appeared just after the battle in Frank Leslie's Magazine. The boy who is represented astride one of the captured guns was James Thorne, a lad of about sixteen years old, a member of Company A and a native of Tennessee. As he sat on the captured cannon and patted it lovingly, he called out to the commander of his company, 'Here it is, Captain.' ...

"When we reached the ridge running parallel with the river before it begins to go northward, it was about sunset. The whole Confederate line had fallen back, leaving a large number of prisoners in our hands."

---Gibson, 78th Pennsylvania, Miller's Brigade

"Yankee Gen. Jeff Davis's Division marched by and over me, and the commanders of the companies would say as they passed me: 'Look out, men, here is a wounded man.' Some of them would step over me carefully, while others would give me a kick and call me a damned rebel, and I was covered with black spots from the bruises."

---Cpl. McKay, 18th Tennessee, Palmer's Brigade

"As the Twentieth Tennessee retreated ... we would load and turn and fire back ..., and when we reached the ground near the fence ..., as I loaded my gun and turned to fire, a minnie ball struck me in the left breast, and I was left there a good portion of the night in the rain. The wound was not so severe, but it cut a furrow about five inches long over my heart."

---McMurray, 20th Tennessee, Preston's Brigade

"I never felt the least frightened until we were ordered back, and then I was (so) badly scared my back itched the whole time, but thank god I escaped untouched."

---Rogers, 1st Florida, Preston's Brigade

"The nearest the (Yankees) ... came to getting me was shooting a hole in my pants and cutting hair off my right temple. I know a peck of balls passed in less than a yard of me. ... The man in front of me got slightly wounded (and) ... the one on my right mortally and the one on my left killed.

"I did not feel any different while under fire than I do at any kind of work. I took 20 deliberate shots, picking my man every time, and one time I saw the man fall, but the others I could not see on account of my smoke. My gun kept choking."

---Ives, 4th Florida, Preston's Brigade

"As our infantry fell back much disordered, but rallying at their old position, our command soon began to receive attention, and under a sharp fire the command, guns and all, were withdrawn to the shelter of ... rising ground. We fell back a hundred or two yards at a time, our guns coming into action at each halt. ...

"The Yankees' three cheers sounded hatefully in my ears after they realized that the attack had failed and would not be renewed."

---Capt. H.B. Clay, Pegram's Cavalry Brigade (dismounted)

"The lines were reformed in the place where the fight commenced and then we had time to count our numbers. In this bloody fight of not more than an hour's duration, Breckenridge's Division had lost more than a thousand men. ... We spent the greater part of the night - it was dark when the fighting ceased - in marching about and in standing picket. ... A cold rain was falling, which put an end to all hope of sleep."

---Cooper, 20th Tennessee, Preston's Brigade

"Guards for the night were being mounted. ... Counting off by tens for vidette duty, it fell to my lot. I had time to wring the water from my socks and get my blanket, which was dry. Wrapping it about my dripping clothes, I went to my post. ... The night was bitter cold. My pants were frozen as far up as the tops of my boots."

---Grainger, 6th Kentucky, Hanson's Brigade

"There was no more fighting that night, only picket firing; our division went to carrying rails and soon had a good line of defense in case of attack. We laid behind it on cornstalks in the rain and mud all night."

---Watson, 25th Illinois, Woodruff's Brigade

"This ground was covered with slain. Wee lay in our wett clothes but i had sent some of the boys back to take blankets from the rebbels who wer killed so wet as i was i had my first sleep for several nights. Some of the boys found plenty to eat in the rebbel haversacks."

---Weir, 25th Illinois, Woodruff's Brigade

(On the Union right flank, near the Nashville Pike:)

"The hungry soldiers cut steaks from the slain horses, and with the scanty supplies that have come forward gather around the fires to prepare supper and talk over the incidents of the day. The prospect seems brighter. We have held the ground and in this last encounter have whipped the enemy. There is more cheerful conversation among the men. ...

"Officers come over from adjoining brigades, hoping to find a little whisky, but learn, with apparent resignation and well-feigned composure, that the canteens have been long empty, that even the private flasks, which officers carry with the photographs of their sweethearts, in a side pocket next to their hearts, are destitute of even the flavor of this article of prime necessity."

---Col. J. Beatty, brigade commander

(While the troops scrounge supper and try to stay warm and dry, surgeons in the field hospitals work late into the night to save the lives of Yankees and Rebels wounded in Breckinridge's charge:)

"About midnight there was a wounded Confederate officer (Capt. Peter Bramlett, 2nd Kentucky, Hanson's Brigade) brought to the field operating tent in which I was ... an assistant surgeon, and he was laid just outside the tent. After many hours, Dr. Walton, of Kentucky, who was in charge, said to us: 'We will not do any more work tonight.'

"Just then we heard an exclamation from this officer, and I insisted that he be brought in and his wounds dressed. This was done, and he asked me if his wounds were fatal. I told him that the chances were greatly against him. He was shot through the chest and through the leg.

"He was carried to a shed nearby and laid on some unbailed cotton.

I gave him some water and brandy. The night was very cold; I got an order for a pair of blankets and placed them over him. ... In the morning ... he was sent to Nashville."

---Dr. F.G. Hickman, U.S. surgeon

"About twelve or one o'clock (Friday night), two Yankee boys who were searching the battle field for a friend came along. They seemed very sorry for me and determined to have me taken to the hospital. ... I was taken to a hospital camp and laid out on the ground, (the attendants) ... thinking I was too near dead to waste time on me. It was ... raining."

---Cpl. McKay, 18th Tennessee, Palmer's Brigade

Retreat

(As dawn breaks Saturday, January 3, 1863, Rebels and Yankees watch each other warily for signs an attack is brewing, but neither Bragg nor Rosecrans feels strong enough to resume the battle:)

"After daylight we made fires and warmed ourselves. It rained all day, but there was not much fighting. ... Our company was on picket part of the day, and laid flat in the mud in a cornfield and kept firing away every chance we got; it was not pleasant, you bet, with bullets whizzing around us all the time either; even behind breastwork a fellow had to lay low for their guns were of long range."

---Watson, 25th Illinois, Woodruff's Brigade

"Being able to hobble around with the aid of a stick, I resolved to get back to the regiment. ... I had not gone far before I came up to a squad of men guarding muskets which had been picked up on the battle field. I had lost my gun during the battle, or, rather, I gave it to a soldier to carry for me as I was going to the rear, and he set it up against a tree and left it. I approached the officer who was in command of the squad, and told him I had lost my gun. He told me to go to the stack and select one for myself. I selected a nice Enfield rifle, nearly new, and took it, and went on."

---Owens, 74th Ohio, Miller's Brigade

(At the Union field hospital where Cpl. McKay had been taken by two compassionate Union soldiers:)

"I lay all day Saturday in the rain without any attention; ... when I would ask (attendants) for water, they would say: 'You don't need water; we will take you to the graveyard after a while.' I did not suffer, however, as I could suck the water out of my coat sleeve as it rained on me."

---Cpl. McKay, 18th Tennessee, Palmer's Brigade

"On arriving at the front, which was in the after part of the day, ... some soldiers of an Indiana regiment ... were preparing supper when I came up. I spoke to them, and asked if they could give a wounded soldier something to eat, as I had eaten nothing since leaving the hospital in the morning. They replied that they did not have much, but would divide with me, and give me something. ... I ate a hard-tack and a small piece of meat, thanked them and then set forward again. ...

"I found the Seventy-fourth near the river. ... That night it rained, and I slept but little. It was a very quiet day compared to what it had been for a few days past. We remained close to the river until near evening. That night some one stole my Enfield."

---Owens, 74th Ohio, Miller's Brigade

"In the evening I rode out to the guns ... at an old gin house (at the extreme left of the line). ... There had been hard fighting (Wednesday) all through the fields and cedar brakes on both sides of the (Wilkerson) pike. The timber was cut up enough apparently to destroy it. ... The dead were lieing thick in the brakes and fence corners.

"I noticed one row of dead men, some 40 or 50 yards long, lieing close side by side, seemingly collected for burial. There must have been a hundred of them, all Yankees. This collection had cleared but a small space - there were numbers of others in less than a hundred yards of this row. The enemy had tried hard to hold this place on the Wilkerson Pike.

"There were but few Confederates, and they lay on their faces, still grasping their guns."

---Brown, Stanford's Mississippi Battery, Stewart's Brigade

"About dark on Saturday, finding that I would not die, I was picked up and laid in a tent out of the rain. During the night two wounded Confederates died in this tent, one of them having fallen across my legs, and lay there several hours."

---Cpl. McKay, 18th Tennessee, Palmer's Brigade

(Bragg counts his casualties and mulls reports that Rosecrans has been reinforced. The Confederate commander concludes his army can neither resume the offensive nor withstand a counterattack:)

"Toward night it was whispered about that we would evacuate Murfreesboro, and, about two hours before ... (dawn Sunday), the retreat commenced. We struggled through the mud till we reached Murfreesboro, and started out on the Wartrace road."

---Cooper, 20th Tennessee, Preston's Brigade

"The troops were marching a good portion of the night and we all knew that we were evacuating the place and to (a) passive enemy at that. At 4 a.m. (Sunday) we harnessed up and moved out on the Shelbyville Pike."

---Brown, Stanford's Mississippi Battery

"It was in the midst of a cold, winter rain, just before daylight (Sunday), ... that Maney's Brigade, the First Tennessee in the rear, waded the river on the retreat to Shelbyville. To undress would be to get our clothes wet anyhow, to say nothing of the difficulty (in putting) on wet boots after they had been taken off. We kept our clothes on. The water was up to our waists. ... In this uncomfortable condition we set out on the march of some twenty-five miles, which we made by the next night."

---Seay, 1st Tennessee, Maney's Brigade

"When (Sunday) ... dawned we were several miles from the Yankees. ... We stopped to rest about dinner time, and I washed my face and hands for the first time in five days."

---Cooper, 20th Tennessee, Preston's Brigade

"(When) we stopped for lunch ... I was sick through and through. Lying down on a log in the sun for rest, I was taken with a chill, which lasted some hours. I was permitted to march at will. Procuring an abandoned horse, I rode all day and stayed in a schoolhouse that night. I was taken with pneumonia and was sent to Wartrace by ambulance, thence to Chattanooga. I remembered nothing after reaching the station until, several days later, I regained consciousness and found myself in the hospital."

---Grainger, 6th Kentucky, Hanson's Brigade

(South of the battlefield, at Beechwood, Katharine Cumming anxiously awaits news of her husband:)

"The fourth day after the battle had begun I was wandering, as usual, aimlessly and restlessly about the ground when I saw a horseman approaching the house, and, hoping he might have some tidings of interest to me, I hastened to intercept him. ... A gaunt and travel-stained-looking soldier ... wearily dismounted, and not till he spoke did I recognize my own husband. ... How I wished he could tell of a wound severe enough to keep him from 'the front' for a while; but not so. ...

"The Confederate army was in orderly retreat, not being followed by Rosecrans, so he had made a detour from the main column to reach Beechwood and see us and hurry us off southward by the next train. The cars might stop running at any moment; the country was full of stragglers; it was a lawless time, and then we ran the risk of falling within the enemy's lines. ... No train went till the next morning. After much persuasion, we prevailed upon (my husband) ... to stay and dry his clothes and partake of a good meal, to have a night's rest from off the ground, and rejoin his command in the morning. ...

"(After he left) we went back to Georgia."

---Katharine Hubbell Cumming

(Near McMinnville, Virginia French realizes Sunday that what had started as a great Confederate victory has turned sour:)

"Many citizens returned from Murfreesboro today - indeed the road has been full of horse men and wagons all afternoon. Gov. Harris, Andrew Ewing, Judge Humphrey and many others ... report ... the Yankees re-inforced, and our men having got off all prisoners and things captured, were retreating in good order to Wartrace and Shelbyville.

They say this - but they will retreat to Chattanooga, as sure as you live - and we will be left here at the mercy of those savages, the Yankees. What is to become of us God only knows."

---L. Virginia French

"Everything quiet in our front. It is reported that the enemy has disappeared. Investigation confirms the report, and the cavalry push into Murfreesboro and beyond."

---Col. J. Beatty, brigade commander

"We ... heard for certain that the rebels had left and were not sorry, either, for we were pretty tired and worn out, too, for we had nothing to eat for three days to amount to anything. Some eat horseflesh, even, being so near starved. I gathered up corn that the mules had left and eat it and was glad to get it."

---Watson, 25th Illinois, Woodruff's Brigade

"The soldiers had a hard time to get something to eat. As much as twenty-five cents was offered for a single hard-tack. Money could not buy rations. They could not be had."

---Owens, 74th Ohio, Miller's Brigade

"During the forenoon the army crosses Stone River, and, with music, banners, and rejoicings, takes possession of the old camps of the enemy. ...

"(Monday) I ride over the battlefield. In one place a caisson and five horses are lying, the latter killed in harness, and all fallen together.

"Nationals and Confederates, young, middle-aged, and old, are scattered over the woods and fields for miles. ...

"We find men with their legs shot off; one with brains scooped out with a cannon ball; another with half a face gone; another with entrails protruding; young Winnegard, of the Third, has one foot off and both legs pierced by grape at the thighs; another boy lies with his hands clasped above his head, indicating that his last words were a prayer.

"Many Confederate sharpshooters lay behind stumps, rails, and logs, shot in the head. A young boy, dressed in the Confederate uniform, lies with his face turned to the sky and looks as if he might be sleeping. ...

"Many wounded horses are limping over the field. ...

"In the evening I met (generals) Rousseau, McCook, and Crittenden. They had been imbibing freely. Rousseau insisted upon my turning back and going with them to his quarters. Crittenden was the merriest of the party. On the way he sang, in a voice far from melodious, ... 'Mary had a little lamb, ...' "

---Col. J. Beatty, brigade commander

The Wounded

(While Bragg and Rosecrans regroup their armies, thousands of wounded Rebels and Yankees are tended in field hospitals, homes and public buildings in and around Murfreesboro:)

"On Monday (Jan. 5) I was given breakfast, the first food offered me, and the first I had eaten since Friday. ... (A) surgeon examined me and decided to amputate my leg; my arm could not be saved. ... I begged them not to cut it off. This attracted the attention of the chief, a big Dutch surgeon, who came and examined me and said: 'Let him alone. If de damn Rebel wants to die, let him go.' ... The young surgeon in charge of the tent was ... very kind to me. ...

"About the 7th or 8th (of January), Casper Freas, a Union, or Yankee sympathizer, ... came with Mrs. R.R. Clemmons in search of her husband. ... I was reported killed ...; so Mr. Freas and Mrs. Clemmons were very much surprised to find me.

"Mr. Freas ... procured a certificate from the surgeon that I was mortally wounded, and with this he got a pass to take me out of the lines. ... Mr. Freas came for me about the 10th ... with a spring wagon and feather bed.

"The young surgeon ... gave me a pair of blankets, a bottle of whisky, some tea, coffee, and sugar; but as soon as the wagon was out of his sight the Yankee guards and camp loafers took ... the whiskey, and the blankets from over me: the other things they did not find, as they were under the feather bed.

"Mr. Freas took me to his home, about ten miles from Murfreesboro, in Wilson County. His family consisted of a wife and six children, and his house had only one large room. I could not understand until afterwards why he would burden himself with a wounded man. He was a Union man and feared the Confederates would take his horses, but he knew that if he had a wounded man in his house, they would not disturb him. He took especially good care of me and no doubt saved my life. ...

"When he got his affairs in order, he sent to Murfreesboro for a squad of men ... to guard him to town ... from where he went to Indiana. ... The night he left me proved to be the most horrible of all my trials.

"He sold all his effects that he could not move to the negroes in the neighborhood. ... The small bed that I was on had been sold to a big negro fellow who lived near, and he promised Mr. Freas that he would stay with me until morning, the family left about midnight.

"The wagons were not out of hearing before the negro began bringing in fence rails to make a fire by putting one end in the fire and the other out on the floor. ... I begged him to desist, but he would not. ... He said he would make me a good fire and then go home. He filled the fireplace with the rails and then left me. I had a fine fire for a time, but did not enjoy it, as I expected the house to burn and me with it. ... Fortunately, the rails were cedar and the fire died out before reaching the floor.

"The next morning, Mr. John M. Cason, hearing from the negroes that Mr. Freas had gone, came over early to see what had become of me. He found me very cold and despondent. He hurried back and got some breakfast and bed clothing for me. He then notified Mr. M.W. Huddleston of my condition, who at once came with wagon and feather bed and took me to his house, near Cainsville, and nursed me until I was able to walk on crutches, some time during the early summer of 1863."

---Cpl. McKay, 18th Tennessee, Palmer's Brigade

(Among the Confederate wounded abandoned in Murfreesboro is Capt. William Campbell of the 1st Arkansas Mounted Rifles. The battle had started just as his mother arrived from Owensboro, Kentucky, with new clothing he had requested. She stays in the city until Bragg retreats, when she learns Campbell is wounded and is in an academy being used as a hospital. A cannonball had killed his horse and shattered the captain's leg, but Campbell had made a tourniquet with his sash and stopped the bleeding:)

"I went into three rooms looking at all the wounded soldiers - perhaps 150 men, then into another room where I found William badly wounded in the leg - about half way between the ankle and knee. The bone was much fractured. It was awful. ...

"I was afraid for two days that his life was in danger and thought his leg would have to be amputated. I ... found Dr. Pendleton of Hartford and he has taken charge of the case. I think he will treat it so as to save the leg but think (William) ... must be lame. He bears it well and tries to be cheerful. ...

"I do not know what he would have done or what he will still do if I were not here, for there are so many wounded - about 800. ... Some were sent off. William and some other officers were not able to be moved or they would not have remained to be prisoners. ...

"The flesh just began last night (Jan. 9) to slough. A large piece of bone is naked this morning and the inflammation seems to be assuaged some. ...

"I am busy from morning till night and from night till morning. I stay all the time with William. The room is very nice and comfortable. I sleep a little sitting in a chair or my head on his cot. The next room is the surgeons' - such as they are - tho they are very gentlemanly but green, green."

---Sara Worthington Kincheloe Campbell

(Campbell's leg had to be amputated, and his only anesthetic was a glass of whiskey. But, he had his mother nearby to nurse him. Most of the wounded had to rely on whatever help was available. The director of the Columbus,

Ohio, branch of the civilian United States Sanitation Commission is one of many Northern volunteers who hurry to Murfreesboro to help with the wounded:)

"We arrived here last Saturday (Jan. 10), after a pleasant ride in an ambulance, from Nashville - thirty miles. ... For fifteen miles nearly every house was burned, and all looked devastation and ruin. One village - Lavergne - was burned and near by were the ruins of our large army train, burned by the rebels on the first day of the battle. Horses and mules burned to death gave one a horrid picture of war. For the remaining fifteen miles, every house was occupied as a hospital, where our poor soldiers are suffering from wounds, and the loss of limbs, and the groans of the dying are heard as you pass. ...

"We have about two thousand wounded (Union soldiers) here and in the vicinity, and all are well cared for. ... The government supplies were good, and the United States Sanitary Commission ... had forwarded sixty or seventy tons of all kinds of clothing, dried and canned fruit, concentrated beef and chickens, etc., necessary for the comfort of the sick and wounded. ... Eight wagon-loads of supplies were sent on Monday, and seven on Wednesday, from Nashville, and a large amount distributed among our four thousand wounded in Nashville.

"It was an exceedingly gratifying sight to see boxes of sanitary goods, at the different hospitals, with the imprint of 'Soldiers' Aid Society, Cleveland,' boxes marked with contents from 'Soldiers' Aid Society, Columbus,' and other places. Our soldiers think, as one said, they come from God's country. ...

"I visited, with (a friend), ... the rebel hospitals under his charge, and found them wanting many things - indeed almost everything to make them comfortable. Men badly wounded were lying upon the hard floor, without straw, because it could not be obtained from us; and the poor men were calling out for something to eat. I asked him why this was so. He replied, 'Because we have not got it to give them.' He was kind and attentive to the men, and was doing all in his power to make them comfortable.

"The other rebel hospitals were in a wretched condition - filthy, and not half cared for by their surgeons. Gangrene was making its appearance from the wounds. There are about fifteen hundred wounded rebels here.

"In a large church, with upper and lower rooms occupied by them, they had only one candle to see to attending several hundred men during the night; and one of our party took some over to them."

---Sessions, Columbus Civilian Sanitary Commission

"Our wounded mostly have been sent to Nashville. The rich were made to give up their soft beds and fine houses for the wounded. ... (Gen.) Mitchell is in command at Nashville. He just drives the Secesh out of their houses and puts our wounded in.

"In Murfreesboro every house is a hospital mostly filled with the worst wounded rebels. The Provo Marshall has been up there for three or four days paroling them. He says there is from five to seven thousand of them. They run all their slightly wounded south on the (railroad) cars as fast as they were wounded. In fact every house through this country is filled with their sick & wounded.

"I was out foraging a day or two since and the Negroes told me there was a sick soldier in Massas house, where is massa, gone south with the army. I went into the house, asked where that sick soldier was. They hesitated but finely said up stairs. Up I went and found and paroled Mr. butternut. He seemed to be very glad. He lived in Arkansas."

---Capt. Philip Welshimer, 21st Illinois, Carlin's Brigade

"The first death in our hospital occurred on (Jan. 5, Monday). ... There were several more deaths within the next fortnight, one of them ... shocking. ... It was a boy from an Indiana regiment, belonging to my own division. ... He told us one day he was not quite eighteen.

"His wound was in the neck, the bullet passing quite through and out behind at the right shoulder, and so injuring the larynx that it was only with difficulty he could speak, even in a whisper. ... Nearly two weeks had passed since that memorable Wednesday, when one morning he told the nurse ... his wound was growing very painful, and if secondary hemorrhage occurred, as was almost certain, he knew that he could not live. ...

"I could see every motion of the poor fellow on his cot directly opposite. Presently I heard a peculiar strangling cough, and looking toward him I saw the nurse bending over him and raising him into a sitting position, while the blood gushed in streams from his mouth, his nostrils, and the external wound in his throat. The surgeon was called instantly; but his endeavors ... were hopeless. ... In less than five minutes the nurse was supporting only a drooping corpse.

"It was a sickening sight, a horrible death. Wounded in much the same spot, how soon might not the end of earth come so to me? I buried my head in my blankets and strove to shut the scene away from my vision; but the picture haunted me, and for days and weeks afterward it would come to me at times, all ghastly and crimson. ...

"After the second week there were fewer deaths in the field-hospitals. There were fewer inmates, too, ... for most of the wounded could bear removal, and were being forwarded to Nashville as rapidly as possible. ... My system yielded much to the violence it had suffered. ... Appetite failed next, and spirits and strength, I could daily feel, were deserting me together. At last Wynne contrived my transfer to Nashville. ... The evening air was freshening chill and wintry when the ambulance stopped before the iron gate of the inclosure of Number Fourteen. ... I was lifted out and borne on a stretcher up into a comfortable, airy room in the second story, ... which now I was not to leave again for more than three long months."

---Hannaford, 6th Ohio, Grose's Brigade

(Dr. Hickman is sent from the Union field hospital near Murfreesboro to an army hospital in Nashville, where he keeps

busy tending the wounded. About Jan. 12 he notices in a newspaper the obituary of the Confederate captain he had treated the night after Breckinridge's charge. From a friend he learns more about the captain's death:)

"Mrs. Payne, ... a frequent visitor at the hospital related to me that she had cared for several Confederate soldiers, one of whom was Capt. Bramlett, who had died at her house. She said that when he was about to die she concluded to remove the coarse blankets and replace them with neater ones; that he caught her hand and said: 'No, do not remove those blankets, for they saved my life at Stone's River. They were placed over me that cold night by the hand of an enemy, but a brother. You may come across him sometime; and if you should, tell him I died under the blankets he placed over me that night.' She sent them to his parents in Paris, Ky."

---Hickman, U.S. surgeon

(James Ellis, who had hopped a train the night of December 31 rather than let a surgeon cut off his wounded arm, finds a refuge about 26 miles south of Murfreesboro:)

"I had relatives, my mother's people, at Shelbyville, to which place I made my painful, weary way. My mother's uncle, Joseph Green, an aged farmer three miles from Shelbyville, although he and his good wife, Aunt Amy, had never seen me, received me as if I had been their own son. ...

"The ladies of the neighborhood, hearing that a wounded soldier from Arkansas was at Uncle Joe Green's, came to see me, and by their kindness and by the care of a country doctor and my dear old aunt my arm was saved."

---Ellis, 4th Arkansas, McNair's Brigade

(A Union officer shot down in the Dec. 30 picket skirmish that got a promotion for Lt. White of the 10th South Carolina meets a less happy fate:)

"Maj. Frank B. Ward of the Fifteenth Pennsylvania Cavalry (had been) ... carried mortally wounded to the house of my father, Dr. J.E. Manson, on the first day of the battle. Maj. Ward had a brother on the Confederate side, who was in this battle, also; and they had been having some amusing correspondence, each saying the other would be his prisoner.

"The major lay wounded for several weeks, when by a sloughing from the main artery of the leg, he bled to death. His brother, the Confederate, came to see him on the day that he died, and they held each other by the hand and recited the Lord's prayer just before the major expired. A brother and sister came down from Michigan, and were at his death bed."

---J.E. Manson, civilian

Index to Eyewitnesses

(' - times quoted on same page)

Bibliography

(Abbreviations: CV - "Confederate Veteran Magazine," followed by volume/page; BL - "Battles and Leaders of the Civil War"; CPA - Chickamauga and Chattanooga National Military Park archives; SB - "Southern Bivouac"; and SRA - Stones River Battlefield archives.)

Beatty, Col. John - 3rd Ohio; "The Citizen Soldier, or, Memoirs of a Volunteer 1861-1863," by Beatty; Cincinnati; Wilstach, Baldwin & Co., Publishers, 1879. Also, "Memoirs of a Volunteer 1861-1863," John Beatty, Harvey S. Ford, editor, W.W. Norton & Co Inc., New York, 1946; courtesy Mrs. Harvey S. Ford.

Berry, John M. - 8th Arkansas; CV 8/73

Brown, A.H. - 13th Tennessee; CV 17/449.

Brown, Sgt. William A. - Stanford's Mississippi Battery; SRA; courtesy Stanford Mississippi Battery, Inc.

Campbell, Sara Worthington Kincheloe - SRA copy of Jan. 10, 1863, letter; courtesy J.A. Barton Campbell.

Canfield, Capt. S.S. - 21st Ohio; "History of the 21st Regiment Ohio Volunteer Infantry in the War of Rebellion," by Canfield; Toledo, Ohio; Vrooman, Anderson and Bateman, printers, 1893, pages 73-75.

Clay, Capt. H.B. - Pegram's Cavalry Brigade; CV 21/589.

Cooper, James L. - 20th Tennessee; CV 33/57ff.

Crittenden, Maj. Gen. Thomas L. - BL vol 3, pages 632ff.

Cumming, Katharine Hubbell; CV 13/410

Dokken, Lars Olsen - 15th Wisconsin; SRA copy of Jan. 10, 1863, letter. Courtesy Mrs. Lawrence Kittleson.

Douglas, Maj. James Postell - Douglas' Battery; "Douglas's Texas Battery, CSA," edited by Lucia Rutherford Douglas, 1966; courtesy Smith County Historical Society, Tyler, Texas.

Eby, Henry Harrison - 7th Illinois Cavalry; SRA copy of extract from "Observations of an Illinois Boy in Battle, Camp and Prisons - 1861 to 1865"; Mendota, Illinois 1910.

Ellis, James W. - 4th Arkansas; CV 17/581.

French (Smith), L. Virginia - Diary, Tennessee State Archives copy, Ms. Div. Ac. No. 73-25. Courtesy Mrs. Henry B. Gilman.

Garner, Sgt. W.A. - 25th Arkansas; SRA copy of June 1, 1897, letter. Courtesy Alice Brock.

Gibson, J.T. - 78th Pennsylvania; "History off the Seventy-Eighth Pennsylvania Volunteer Infantry," edited by Gibson, 1905.

Grainger, Gervis D. - 6th Kentucky; "Four Years With the Boys in Gray," by Grainger; Franklin, Kentucky, 1902.

Green, John - 9th Kentucky; "Johnny Green of the Orphan Brigade, The Journal of a Confederate Soldier," edited by A.D. Kirwan; copyright 1956 University of Kentucky Press. Courtesy of University of Kentucky Press.

Hannaford, Ebenezer - 6th Ohio; SRA copy from "Harper's New Monthly Magazine," 1863-64, pages 260-264.

Hickman, Dr. F.G. - CV 2/356.

Holloway, Capt. E.S. - 41st Ohio; SRA copy of letter dated Jan. 9, 1863; also, "The Forty-first Ohio Veteran Volunteer Infantry in the War of the Rebellion," by Robert T. Kimberly and Ephriam S. Holloway, Cleveland, Ohio, W.R. Smellie Printer, 1897.

Horrall, Capt. S.F. - 42nd Indiana. CV 16/63 and "History of the Forty-Second Indiana Volunteer Infantry," by Horrall, 1892.

Hutcherson, Joseph, 3rd Georgia Battalion; CV 16/391.

Ives, Washington Mackey - 4th Florida; "The Florida Genealogist," Vol. 8, No. 4, Summer 1985, pages 98ff; courtesy Kenneth and Helen Ives.

Jackman, Jno. S. - 9th Kentucky (CS); SB, vol. III, pages 295-299.

Jones, P.R. - 10th Texas Cavalry (dismounted); CV 31/341.

Kniffin, Lt. Col. Gilbert C. - Gen. Crittenden's staff; BL vol. 3, pages 630-631.

Magee, Cpl. John Euclid - Stanford's Mississippi Battery; courtesy Duke University's manuscript collection, William R. Perkins Library.

Manson, J.E. - CV 3/239.

McKay, Cpl. W.L. - 18th Tennessee; CV 34/245.

McMurray, W.J. - 20th Tennessee; CV 6/123.

M'Dearman - 12th Tennessee; CV 9/306.

Mitchell, James B. - 34th Alabama; SRA copy.

Moody, Col. Granville - 74th Ohio; "A Life's Restrospect, Autobiography of Rev. Granville Moody, D.D.," edited by Rev. Sylvester Weeks. Cincinnati: Curts & Jennings. New York: Eaton and Maris. 1890 Cranston & Stowe.
Moon, G.B. - CV 7/119
Mullet, Samuel - 51st Ohio; SRA copy of letter reprinted from unidentified local paper in "Newcomerstown News," page 4A, Dec. 13, 1972.
Neal, Ralph J. - 20th Tennessee; CV 7/70ff.
Otey, W.N. Mercer - CV 7/550ff.
Owens, Ira S. - 74th Ohio; "Greene County Soldiers in the Late War, Being a History of the Seventy-Fourth O.V.I.," by Owens. Dayton, Ohio. Christian Publishing House Print, 1884.
Pepper, Alexander C. - 59th Illinois; "Memoirs of the Civil War," by Alexander Campbell Pepper, courtesy Dean C. Anderson, editor. 1987.
Pickett, Col. W.D. - CV 16/451ff.
Pirtle, Alfred - 1st Michigan Artillery, SB vol 2, June 1886-May 1887.
Ridley, B.L. - CV 11/65.
Robuck, J.E. - 29th Mississippi; "My Own Personal Experience and Observation as a Soldier in the Confederate Army During the Civil War, 1861-1865," no date; courtesy of 1970 reprint by Burke's Book Store in Memphis, TN.
Rogers, William D. - 1st Florida; SRA copy Jan. 22, 1863, letter; courtesy John Segrest.
Seay, Samuel - 1st Tennessee; SRA copy of extract from SB June-May 1885-86, pages 156ff.
Sessions - Columbus Civilian Sanitary Commision; letter quoted in Ira S. Owens' memoirs.
Silsby, Amandus - 24th Wisconsin; SRA copy of letter dated Feb. 8, 1863.
Smith, J. Morgan - 32nd Alabama; SRA copy Jan. 17, 1863, letter; courtesy Robert Ragland.
Suman, Col. I.C.B. - 9th Indiana, "Deeds of Valor," Walter Frederick Beyer, Detroit, Michigan, the Perrien-Keydel Co., 1903.
Sweet, S. Emory - 9th Tennessee; CV 20/515.
Thruston, Capt. Gates P. - McCook's ordnance officer; "Personal Recollections of the Battle of Stone's River, Tenn." published in Nashville, Tennessee. From a paper read before the Ohio Commandery of Loyal Legion, Oct. 3, 1906, in Cincinnati, OH.
Tunnell, Lt. J.T. - 14th Texas; CV 16/574.
Vaughan, Col. A.J. - 13th Tennessee; "Personal Record of the Thirteenth Regiment, Tennessee Infantry," by Vaughan, 1897; courtesy Burke's Book Store, Memphis, TN.
Walker, I.C. - Adjutant general, Manigault's Brigade; CV 15/263 and 34/46.
Watkins, Sam R. - 1st Tennessee; "Co. 'Aytch' First Tennessee Regiment, or a Side Show of the Big Show," by Watkins; Cumberland Presbyterian Publishing House, Nashville, Tenn., 1882.
Watson, James G. - 25th Illinois; "Middletown Yank's Journey to War and Back," compiled and published by Gerald J. Miller, Champaign, Ill. 1985. Courtesy of Mr. Miller.
Weir, James K. - 25th Illinois; CPA copies of letters dated Jan 8 and 21, 1863.
Welch, Sgt. Samuel - 51st Ohio; SRA copy "A Sketch of Movements of the Fifty-First Ohio Volunteer Infantry," in 1980 reprint of "Combination Atlas Map of Tuscarawas County Ohio, 1908," Gordon Printing, Strasbourg, Ohio. Courtesy of Tuscarawas County Genealogical Society and Mrs. Jane W. Blount.
Welshimer, Capt. Philip - 21st Illinois; SRA copies Dec. 28, 1862, Jan. 4, 7, 11 and 17, 1863, letters; courtesy Illinois State Historical Society,
Whitehead, Rev. John M - 15th Indiana, SRA copy from "Deeds of Valor," Walter Frederick Beyer, Detroit, Michigan, the Perrien-Keydel Co., 1903.
Widney, Sgt. Maj. Lyman - 34th Illinois; SRA copy of diary extracts. Courtesy of Miriam McGlothlin Piercy.

(General References:)

"Autumn of Glory," Thomas L. Connelly, 1971, Louisiana State University Press.

"Campaigns and Battles of the Sixteenth Regiment, Tennessee Volunteers, in the War Between the States," by Thomas A. Head; 1895.

"Letters from the Front; A Union 'Preacher' Regiment (74th Ohio) in the Civil War," by Theodore W. Blackburn; Press of Morningside Bookshop, Dayton, Ohio.

"Stones River - Bloody Winter in Tennessee," by James Lee McDonough, University of Tennessee Press, 1980.

"The Army of Tennessee," Stanley F. Horn, 1941, University of Oklahoma Press.

The Battle of Franklin

"Eyewitnesses at the Battle of Franklin," the first in this series, draws on accounts by almost 50 soldiers, women and children who witnessed the terror and the gallantry of Hood's bloody blunder on Nov. 30, 1864.

The eyewitnesses include a little girl who, with her family, cringed in the cellar of the battered Carter House, where Rebels almost broke the Yankee line.

An excited 15-year-old boy tells of climbing tree limbs and onto rooftops to watch the Confederate attack - until bullets started flying too close for comfort. After the battle, he helped tend the wounded and gathered vegetables from the countryside to feed them.

The Johnny Reb who would be editor of "Confederate Veteran" magazine after the war describes the mortal wounding of Gen. Otho Strahl in the twilight's vicious trench fighting.

A Yankee captain whose command was overwhelmed vividly recalls running for his life and barely making it over friendly breastworks as a Rebel fires at him.

These first-person accounts, and many more, bring the Battle of Franklin alive. After reading "Eyewitnesses at the Battle of Franklin" you will know what it was like for the Yankees and Rebels who fought there.